D1647928

WHAT'S COOKING
MADISON?
BY THE SEA

A Diverse Collection of Recipes from
Madison Residents, Restaurants and Inns

Diane Gardner
Kim Castaldo

Photographs by Kelley McMahon

Design by Lisa Kronauer

Copyright 2005

Diane Gardner

Kim Castaldo

www.whatscookingmadison.com

Photographs by

Kelley McMahon

copyright 2005

Design by

Lisa Kronauer

All rights reserved. No part of this book may be copied or reproduced by any means, stored in a

retrieval system or transmitted in any form or by any means, electronic, mechanical,

photocopying, or otherwise, without the prior permission of the publisher.

Published by

Jostens, Commerical Publications

ISBN 0-9773675-0-9

WHAT'S COOKING
MADISON?

BY THE SEA

Welcome

Over the past few months we have been
busy talking with restaurants, inns and many residents of Madison.
We have been listening to family stories and testing recipes!
We have had the opportunities to enjoy the recipes
that have been so generously shared for this cook book.
The ideas of family and easy cooking are what this book represents.
As you read, you will feel the love that has been shared by so many.
These recipes are simple and delicious and are presented in
the original recipe form in which we received them.
The uniqueness of each recipe adds to the beauty of the book.
Tradition was a big flavor on our thoughts and ideas for
What's Cooking Madison. Every family has traditions.
Traditions that they repeat year after year.
We have included many recipes that families of
Madison prepare for special holidays in their homes.
As you read through our book, we hope that you
will find wonderful ideas and recipes that you can
include in your own holiday traditions!!!!!!
Happy Cooking, Diane and Kim.

TABLE OF CONTENTS

MADISON

GREAT STARTERS

Tomato and Mozzarella Martini

Cauliflower Fritters

Buffalo Chicken Wing Dip

Traditional Polish Pierogies

Calamari Marinara

Scallops Wrapped in Pancetta

Chicken Liver and Onion Paté

Stuffed Quahog Clams

Sausage Wontons

Catie's Leeks and Mushrooms in Puffed Pastry

Dino's Italian Egg Rolls

Lynch's Coconut Shrimp

Lamb Chops with Rosemary

Liz's Crab Cakes

Clams Casino

Peggy's Toasted Bacon Triangles

Mike's Marvelous Stuffed Mushrooms

Fruit and Cheese Platter

GREAT STARTERS

TOMATO AND MOZZARELLA MARTINI

4 pounds vine-ripened
   tomatoes
salt and freshly ground
   pepper, to taste
16 small, fresh
   mozzarella balls
16 cherry tomatoes
fresh basil leaves, cut
   into thin strips

Chill 4 martini glasses. Peel, seed and chop vine-ripened tomatoes. Salt and pepper tomatoes. Place tomatoes in a sieve suspended over a bowl and refrigerate for several hours. As the tomatoes release their juices, the liquid will be almost clear and loaded with flavor. Thread a cherry tomato and mozzarella ball onto each of the 16 skewers. Place 4 skewers into each glass, divide tomato liquid among the 4 glasses. Sprinkle basil strips over the skewers. Serve promptly.

Shared by Phyllis Carroll

CAULIFLOWER FRITTERS

This is a very simple and delicious appetizer to serve either before a family dinner or at a cocktail party. Kids love it as well as adults. You can prep everything ahead of time and the last step is easy. Enjoy!

Bring large pot of water to boil. Add liberal amount of salt. Blanche cauliflower in boiling, salted water until just tender. Drain and set aside to cool. This can be done ahead of time.

Meanwhile, mix Bisquick with the egg and enough water to form a fairly thin batter, about the consistency of heavy cream (thinner than for pancakes). Heat oil in large skillet and when hot, dip cauliflower pieces in batter and, working in batches, fry until golden brown on all sides.

Drain on paper towels, sprinkle with salt and serve hot!

Shared by Lisa Leonardi

1   head cauliflower cut into florets
1   cup Bisquick
1   egg
1   cup water
salt
¼   cup vegetable oil

BUFFALO CHICKEN WING DIP

2 whole boneless, skinless chicken breasts

2 8 ounce packages cream cheese, softened

1 8 ounce package cheddar cheese, shredded

1 jar Marie's Blue Cheese Dressing

1 bottle chicken wing sauce (I use Frank's)

The night before, bake chicken and shred into pieces. Spread cream cheese over it. Pour entire jar of blue cheese dressing over that and then top with the shredded cheese. Refrigerate overnight.

Bake at 350° until cheese melts. Serve with tortilla chips and wing sauce.

Shared by Annie Auerbach

There isn't a story for this recipe, I just like it! I am originally from the Buffalo area and grew up eating chicken wings. This is a great dip that combines all the flavors.

TRADITIONAL POLISH PIEROGIES

Every year as far back as I can remember I used to join all my siblings and cousins around my grama's kitchen table making a huge mess that finally ended with the most desired delicious cheese treats —pierogi.

About a week before Easter, Christmas and any other special family event, we would gather around my grama's table and all help in the making of our famous pierogi. They would be the center of our table and the kid's most favorite part of the meal. I was never sure if I really loved the taste of them, or loved the making of the memories more. Every Polish family knows of this delicious holiday staple, but it truly is a fun family experience to make together.

Mound flour on kneading board and make a hole in center. Drop eggs into hole and cut into flour with knife. Add salt and water and knead until firm. Let rest for 10 minutes covered with a warm towel. Divide dough into halves and roll thin.

Cut circles with a large biscuit cutter. Place a small spoonful of filling a little to one side on each round of dough. Moisten edge with water; fold over and press edges together firmly. Be sure they are well sealed to prevent filling from running out. Drop pierogi into salted boiling water. Cook gently for 3-5 minutes. Let stand. Lift out of water carefully with perforated spoon.

The filling can be farmer's cheese mixed with cream cheese. You can add onions that have been lightly fried in butter. Sometimes we would use mashed potatoes mixed with farmers cheese for a filling, and another variation is sauteed cabbage with onions. When the pierogies are boiled we coat them with onions that have been fried in butter. We always garnish them with sour cream. We love to have them fried when having leftovers!

Another variation for the summertime that grama would make is a filling of blueberries with a bit of sugar and lemon juice. Good Luck!!

Shared by Cindi Gardner

2	eggs
2	cups flour
½	cup water
½	teaspoon salt

Nestled on the corner of Bradley Road and Wall Street, Bradley and Wall is a local gourmet deli that specializes in Italian cooking. Owner Joe does most of his own cooking. They also offer an assortment of specialty pizzas, including a white clam pizza.

CALAMARI MARINARA

¾ pound calamari, wash and cut into small pieces

3 garlic cloves, chopped

3 basil leaves, chopped

3 tablespoons olive oil

1 shot glass of white wine

1 cup marinara sauce

salt and pepper, to taste

2 tablespoons parsley, chopped

Heat garlic cloves in sauce pan coated with olive oil on medium high. Sauté until garlic is golden brown, adding the basil leaves.

Add calamari and sauté for 2 minutes. Add shot of wine, sauté for 30 seconds. Add marinara sauce, salt and pepper to taste. Add parsley and simmer on low heat for 20 minutes. Serve with hot crusty bread!

Shared by Joe Coniglialo, owner of Bradley and Wall Gourmet Foods

SWIM AREA FLAG KEY

OPEN: Swim area supervised by lifeguard.

WARNING: No lifeguard on duty

CLOSED: Swim area temporarily unsafe.

SCALLOPS WRAPPED IN PANCETTA

1 pound Boars Head pancetta, thinly sliced

1 pound large scallops

wasabi ginger sauce (Star Fish Market in Guilford has great sauce)

rosemary skewers, soaked in water for 1 hour

Wrap scallop with pancetta. Thread through rosemary skewers. Marinate with wasabi ginger sauce.

Cook on grill 2 minutes on each side, until golden brown. Serve warm.

Shared by Liz Wallack

CHICKEN LIVER AND ONION PATÉ

2 large onions, chopped

½ stick butter

1 pound chicken livers, diced

2 garlic cloves, chopped

salt and pepper, to taste

Port wine

Sauté onions in butter until golden. Add chicken livers and garlic to pan. Sauté the mixture until the livers are cooked but not browned. Season the mixture highly with pepper and salt and put in a blender. Gradually add Port wine to taste. Chill.

This is always a hit at parties!!

Shared by Dottie Cahill and Cari Sweitzer

Scallops Wrapped in Pancetta

STUFFED QUAHOG CLAMS

Wash and clean clams thoroughly, shuck clams and reserve all the juice and save the clam shells. Put clams in a food processor, and pulse until chunky. Set aside.

Mix crushed garlic, olive oil and bread crumbs, butter, Tabasco, fresh oregano and parsley. Add chunky clams and the reserved juice until mixture is semi-soupy, but a little thick.

Scoop clam mixture into clean clam shells and bake at 375° for about 25 minutes.

Shared by Denise Gravina

1 dozen large quahog clams, cleaned, shucked (reserve juice and save shells)
2 cloves fresh garlic, crushed
3 tablespoons olive oil
1½ cups bread crumb
½ stick butter, melted
1 dash Tabasco
1 teaspoon fresh oregano
1 teaspoon fresh parsley

Having spent many summer vacations on Martha's Vineyard over the years, our family has found a favorite clamming spot. At low tide entire Gravina family (uncl aunts, grandparents, cousins,...) could be found elbow deep in mud or with a rake in shallow water search ing for clams of all shapes a sizes. At the close of the dig, the family would trek back home to sort, clean, and feas on a variety of clam dishes. The stuffed quahog recipe is personal, simple favorite. Enjoy!

SAUSAGE WONTONS

In a large skillet, brown sausage over medium high heat breaking up chunks with fork. Remove sausage and let drain on paper towels (squeeze out as much grease as possible). Discard grease from skillet. Return sausage to skillet, add salsa, cheeses and green chiles. Simmer about 5 minutes until mixture thickens. Remove from heat and cool.

Brush mini muffin cups with olive oil. Press 1 wonton wrapper into each muffin cup and fill each wrapper with 1 generous tablespoon of cooled sausage mixture (you can stop at this point and chill for 4 hours). Bake at 350° until edges begin to brown, about 10 minutes. Transfer from muffin cups to baking sheet. Bake until bottoms are crisp, about 10 minutes. Transfer to serving platter and garnish with green onions. Serve warm. Cook time 20 minutes.

Shared by Nicki Cox

¾ **pound Italian sausage, casings removed**

½ **cup medium salsa**

½ **cup Monterey Jack cheese, shredded**

1 **cup sharp cheddar cheese, shredded**

2 **ounces green chiles, diced**

24 **wonton skins or wrappers**

green onions, for garnish

CATIE'S LEEKS AND MUSHROOMS IN PUFFED PASTRY

1   puff pastry sheet,
    Pepperidge Farm
1   large (or two small)
    leeks, cleaned and
    sliced thin
5   ounces fresh
    mushrooms, sliced
1   clove garlic, crushed
2   tablespoons butter
1   cup Imported
    Finlandia Swiss
    cheese, shredded

Defrost pastry sheet and open it to lay flat, pinching the folds together. Sauté sliced leeks, mushrooms and garlic in butter until soft. Spread leek mixture over pastry sheet, within ½ inch on all sides. Sprinkle cheese over leek and mushroom mixture.

Roll pastry into a log shape, pinching ends closed. Brush with egg wash and bake at 400° for approximately 30 minutes, or until golden brown.

Shared by Barbara Gibbons

This is a great hors d' oeuvr
I have served this at many
different occasions, and it is
always a hit. It is simple to
prepare and every time I ma
it someone asks for the recip
Now everyone will have the
opportunity to make it. Enjo

DINO'S ITALIAN EGG ROLLS

Remove sausage from casing and crumble. Sauté and drain off extra oil. Prepare Dino's broccoli rabe (see page 62). Chop broccoli and toss with cooked sausage. Mix together and test taste. Add seasoning, salt, pepper, and hot red pepper flakes.

Fill middle of spring rolls generously with sausage mixture. Turn the ends of spring roll in and roll. Heat oil in deep fry pan to medium to high heat. Drop in 2-3 rolls at a time and fry until golden brown and crispy.

Shared by Dino Landino of Balladino's

6　hot Italian sausages

1　bunch broccoli rabe

salt and pepper, to taste

hot red pepper flakes

1　package spring roll wrappers

peanut oil or canola oil, for frying

LYNCH'S COCONUT SHRIMP

Mix 1 cup flour, egg, beer, salt and pepper into a batter. Dredge shrimp in half cup flour, dip in batter, and roll in coconut to cover. Deep fry shrimp at 350° for 3-5 minutes (do so in small batches). Season with salt and pepper. Serve warm with side of sauce.

Shared by Lynch's Restaurant

Sauce:

½   cup orange
      marmalade

2   tablespoons
      horseradish

mix sauce together and
      serve with shrimp

12   medium shrimp,
       peeled and deveined

1½ cups flour

1   egg

½   cup beer (any kind)

1   cup coconut, shredded

salt and pepper, to taste

oil for frying

LAMB CHOPS WITH ROSEMARY

1   package Australian
     lamb chops, sliced
     individually
fresh rosemary, chopped
freshly ground pepper
kosher salt
olive oil
whole sprigs of rosemary

Mix rosemary with kosher salt and pepper. Add a little oil to make a paste.

Rub each chop with mixture.

Grill over high heat about 2 minutes on each side. Arrange on platter with fresh sprigs of rosemary and serve! Easy and delicious

Shared by Diane Gardner

This is a very special appetize[r] that can also be served as a dinner. I use Australian lamb chops and always get them fr[om] Star Fish Market. They have the best! I have also made lar[ge] platters of chops and served th[em] as a finger food. They are always the first thing to go!!

LIZ'S CRAB CAKES

This is a family favorite. My daughter Rachael loves crab cakes, so I made this up one day for her. Now I make them quite often. I have served them at cocktail parties. I just adjust the size of the crab cake to fit the event. Enjoy!

Combine all ingredients, except last two. Refrigerate for 1 hour and up to 24 hours in advance. Mound mixture into cakes, approximately the size of your palm. Pat into breadcrumbs to cover both sides. Sauté in butter until light brown on both sides. Finish cooking in oven. Bake for 8-10 minutes.

Shared by Liz Wallack

1   pound crabmeat
2   tablespoons red onion, diced
¼   cup red pepper, minced
¼   cup yellow pepper, minced
2   teaspoons fresh lemon juice
1   garlic clove, crushed
1   teaspoon mustard
1   cup bread crumbs
2   teaspoons fresh parsley
½   cup mayonnaise
Worcestershire sauce, to taste
Old Bay seasoning, to taste
salt and pepper, to taste
1   cup breadcrumbs
2   tablespoons butter

CLAMS CASINO

2 dozen clams, ready
   for stuffing
¼ onion, finely chopped
½ stick of butter, add
   more as needed to
   make moist stuffing
¼ cup red pepper, finely
   chopped
¼ cup green pepper,
   finely chopped
Italian bread crumbs
2 splashes of white wine
lemon juice, to taste
Worcestershire sauce, to
   taste
salt and pepper, to taste
8 pieces bacon, cooked
   medium crispy

Sauté butter, onion and peppers. Mix with bread crumbs, white wine, lemon juice, Worcestershire, salt and pepper. Fill each clam with mixture and top with chopped bacon.

Bake at 350° for 5 minutes, or until heated throughout.

Shared by Laura Downes

This is a quick and easy recipe. Living on the shore, seafood is always fresh, so this is a favorite appetizer. I get my clams from Star Fish Market in Guilford, and they are always fantastic!

PEGGY'S TOASTED BACON TRIANGLES

This is a fabulous appetizer that I make often when friends drop in unexpectedly. It's easy to whip together and the ingredients are always on hand!

Mix bacon, mayonnaise and scallions in food processor. Toast bread very lightly, until just starting to turn light brown. Cut each piece of toast into two triangles. Coat one side of each triangle with the mayonnaise mixture. Brown under broiler until golden. Serve promptly.

Shared by Peggy Delano

10 pieces white bread, trimmed of crust
½ pound bacon, cooked crisp and broken into pieces
2 tablespoons mayonnaise
5 fresh, washed scallions, chopped fine
pinch of pepper

MIKE'S MARVELOUS STUFFED MUSHROOMS

This is a recipe I created over 25 years ago. They are a hit wherever I bring them!

In a food processor, pulse bread crumbs, ham, pepper and parmesan. Warm butter in a heavy skillet. Cook bread crumb mixture in skillet for a few minutes over medium heat until mixture starts to bind together. Line cookie sheet with mushrooms, open end facing up. Place 1 tablespoon of mixture into each mushroom. Top each mushroom with a sprinkle of parmesan and a drizzle of olive oil. Bake for 15-20 minutes at 350°. Serve warm.

Shared by Michael Delano

1 pound buttonball mushrooms, washed, stems removed
½ cup bread crumbs
10 slices good prosciutto ham, chopped
1 roasted pepper, deseeded and chopped
¼ cup parmigiano reggiano cheese
2 tablespoons butter
olive oil

FRUIT AND CHEESE PLATTER

Fruit suggestions:
fresh pineapple, chunks
bunches of green and
    purple grapes, seedless
figs, sliced 4 ways
large strawberries, whole
    with greens on
raspberries
blueberries
watermelon, small slices
    and/or chunks
pears, sliced
apples, sliced
grape tomatoes

Arranging a fruit and cheese platter is fun and very easy. Make sure that you choose fruits that are nice, ripe and in season. The rest is just cutting the fruit and arranging on the platter. Large clusters of grapes and stacks of crackers give height. Large chunks of cheese fill in the bottom of the platter. Then sprinkle loose berries around to fill in empty spaces on the platter.

Add your favorite fruits, cheeses and crackers and enjoy!

Cheese suggestions:
sharp cheddar
boursin cheese
English stilton
dill havarti
brie
baby Swiss

Fruit and Cheese Platter

SOUPS, SALADS AND SAUCES

Avocado and Mango Salsa
Grilled Peach Salsa
Mango and Black Bean Salsa
Coconut and Lime Salsa
Escarole and Beans
Chilled Apple Soup
Strawberry Soup
Dino's Antipasto
Cabbage and Sausage Soup
Japanese Cabbage Salad
Russian Cucumber Salad
Lemon Chive Potato Salad
Compote Salad with Grilled Chicken and Fruit
Seared Shrimp with Lemon Pepper Vinaigrette
Zuppa Maritata–Wedding Soup
Grilled Vegetable Salad
Summer Tomato Stack
Barbara's Flank Steak Marinade
Mustard Sauce for Tomatoes
Raspberry Vinaigrette Dressing and Salad
Beet and Grapefruit Salad
Dungeness Crab Ceviche
Oodles o' Noodles
Szechuan Chicken Salad
Broccoli Salad
Joe's Fish Stock
Bob's Flank Steak Marinade

SOUPS, SALADS AND SAUCES

AVOCADO AND MANGO SALSA

2 avocados
3 tablespoons lime juice
1 mango
1 small seedless cucumber, diced
2 scallions, sliced thin
¼ cup olive oil
3 tablespoons cilantro, chopped
salt and pepper, to taste

Peel and cut avocados into ¾-inch cubes. In a small bowl, toss gently with lime juice.

Peel mango and cut into ¾-inch cubes. Add mango and remaining ingredients to avocado. Toss gently, being careful not to smash avocado. Season with salt and pepper. Serve within the hour or store in airtight container, refrigerate up to 3 hours.

Shared by Lisa Kronauer

A good trick with mangoes is to cut them in half crosswise with the pit, then cut diagonally, on both diagonals across the section you cut from from the pit. Invert the mango, then slice the mango from the rind.

GRILLED PEACH SALSA

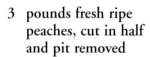

3 pounds fresh ripe peaches, cut in half and pit removed
1 tablespoon sugar
1 tablespoon fresh lime juice
¼ teaspoon salt
½ cup golden raisins

Sprinkle cut sides of peaches with sugar. Cook peaches on grill for approximately 6 minutes or until browned (Use Reynolds Wrap Release Non-Stick Foil Liners on grill so peaches won't slide through the grill grates). Cool peaches on a plate, cut peaches into ½-inch pieces. In a bowl, combine peaches, lime juice, salt and raisins.

Serve promptly, this makes about 4 cups of salsa.

Shared by Charlie Elliott

This salsa is fabulous in the summer when peaches are in abundance. Grilling the peaches makes a huge difference in the taste...we especially like it served with chicken or white fish.

MANGO AND BLACK BEAN SALSA

Combine all ingredients together and chill. Serve this with swordfish, tuna or grilled chicken.

2 ripe mangos, peeled and diced
1 can black beans, drained
1 small red onion, chopped small
1 large handful of fresh cilantro, chopped
½ lime, freshly squeezed

COCONUT AND LIME SALSA

In a large bowl, combine the cherry tomatoes and grated coconut with the chopped basil (always use fresh basil for the best flavor), and seedless cucumber. Add the red chili pepper and toss all of these together.

At this point you can refrigerate until you are ready to serve. Just before serving, toss in the olive oil, salt and freshly ground pepper and lime juice. Taste and adjust seasonings to your liking.

16 cherry tomatoes, quartered
½ fresh coconut, grated (substitute with flaky bag coconut)
12 fresh basil leaves, chopped
1 small seedless cucumber, chopped
1 red chili, sliced thin
1 tablespoon olive oil
2 limes, juiced
salt and pepper, to taste

ESCAROLE AND BEANS

5   cloves of garlic,
    finely chopped

8   tablespoons olive oil

2   sticks pepperoni,
    coarsely chopped

2   cups chicken broth
    (or water)

2   heads of escarole,
    well cleaned and cut
    into shreds

1   can white cannellini
    beans

In large saucepan, heat oil over medium heat. Add garlic and pepperoni and saute 2-3 minutes, until golden brown. Add broth and escarole and simmer until escarole has cooked down. Cover and continue to simmer 20 minutes, while stirring frequently. Add beans. Season to taste with salt and pepper. Serve with warm, crusty bread.

Shared by Kristin Crudo

This is an old family recipe I received from my dear friend's mother, Andrea Paolillo, who has since pass away. It has become a favorite in our home and I think of her every time I ma it. I am happy I can dedica this recipe to her.

This soup recipe comes from my Aunt Viv in Massachusetts.
She served this for many years while we enjoyed the
Thanksgiving holiday at her home.

CHILLED APPLE SOUP

In a large saucepan, combine 10 apples (not peeled), water, apple cider, sugar and cinnamon sticks. Over medium high heat, bring to a boil. Cover and reduce, simmer for approximately 50 minutes or until apples fall apart. Remove saucepan from heat and let cool to room temperature. Scrape pulp from peels and return pulp to cooking liquid. Cover saucepan with plastic wrap and chill overnite. Discard cinnamon sticks. Puree mixture and place back in saucepan, stir in half and half, orange juice, lemon juice and Grand Marnier. Cover with plastic wrap and chill another 4 hours. Serve chilled and sprinkle with 2 red delicious apples, diced.

Shared by Aunt Kelley

10 medium red delicious apples, cored, and quartered (not peeled)

2¼ cups water

1¼ cups fresh apple cider

¾ cup of sugar

2 whole cinnamon sticks

2 cups half and half

1¼ cups orange juice

2 tablespoons lemon juice

2 medium red delicious apples, peeled, cored and diced

6 tablespoons Grand Marnier

STRAWBERRY SOUP

2 cups strawberries, sliced
1 cup sour cream
1 cup half and half
¼ cup sugar
½ teaspoon vanilla extract

This soup turns out best if strawberries are used in season. Be sure to clean strawberries with cold water to remove any dirt or chemicals. Remove all stems and slice strawberries into pieces. Put strawberries and all other ingredients in a blender or food processor. Blend until mixed and soup is a creamy mixture without lumps. Chill soup in refrigerator. Serve chilled with whole strawberries as a garnish. Top with a sprig of cilantro and a dollop of cream.

Shared by Susan Muckle

DINO'S ANTIPASTO

Drain mozzerella ball. Chop the olives, artichoke hearts, red peppers, sopressata and tomatoes in half. Dice the eggplant and add to mixing bowl. Chop the fresh basil and add salt and pepper. Sprinkle in olive oil and mix all ingredients together, and serve.

Shared by Dino Landino of Balladino's

Fresh mozzarella balls
Green and red olives
Artichoke hearts
Roasted red peppers
Sopressata (salami)
Provolone cheese, chunks
Grape tomatoes
Marinated eggplant
Olive oil and fresh basil
salt and pepper, to taste

CABBAGE AND SAUSAGE SOUP

This is a wonderful cold weather soup, a favorite in my house. I always serve this with thick slices of dill bread, see page 146 for recipe. It is very easy to make and will warm you right up!

Boil sausage to release some of the fat, remove skin and crumble sausage in a large pot. Cook cabbage, onion and garlic in oil for 15 minutes. Add remaining ingredients (except sugar and vinegar) to pot. Cook on low to medium heat for approximately 30 minutes. Fifteen minutes prior to serving mix in sugar and vinegar serve warm.

Shared by Audrey Weber

2	pounds sweet Italian sausage
1	large can tomato puree
1	head cabbage, shredded
2	large onions, chopped
4	garlic cloves, chopped
¼	cup olive oil
1	small can chicken and beef broth
1	large can chicken broth
1½	teaspoons cumin
1½	teaspoons oregano
¼	teaspoon allspice
¼	cup brown sugar
¼	cup vinegar

JAPANESE CABBAGE SALAD

1   large head of Chinese cabbage, chopped

3   green onions, chopped

1   package oriental Top Ramen noodles or other oriental dried curly noodle

¼   cup butter

⅓   cup sesame seeds

4   ounce almonds, slivered

Dressing:

1   tablespoon soy sauce

⅓   cup vegetable oil

¼   teaspoon sesame oil

¼   cup unseasoned rice wine vinegar

⅓   cup sugar

Crush dried curly noodles and brown them with sesame seeds and almonds in melted butter. Remove from pan and set aside to cool. Chop cabbage and green onions. Mix well in serving bowl. Toss cooled mixture with chopped cabbage and green onions. Add dressing when ready to serve.

Option:
Add cooked chicken to make the salad a main dish.

Shared by Kris Moss

A simple yet delicious salad perfect for a casual gathering, or picnic at the beach!

RUSSIAN CUCUMBER SALAD

My mother's side of the family is Russian and Polish, and this is a recipe passed down from them. It's a great cold dish in the summer when cucumbers are fresh and plentiful.

Cut cucumbers lengthwise, remove seeds. Slice each half of cucumber in crescent shape slices. Cover with white wine vinegar and salt, let marinate for 30 minutes.

Drain cucumbers and pat dry. Mix in eggs, sour cream and spices. Refrigerate and serve cold.

Shared by Susan Ciotti Wivell

4	cucumbers, peeled and deseeded
1	cup white vinegar
2	teaspoons sea salt
2	hard boiled eggs, chopped
1	cup sour cream
1	teaspoon dill weed
1	teaspoon white pepper
1	teaspoon mustard
3	teaspoons horseradish

LEMON CHIVE POTATO SALAD

3   **pounds small red potatoes**

1   **lemon, squeezed**

1   **teaspoon lemon zest, grated**

1½ **tablespoons olive oil**

½   **teaspoon sugar**

1   **teaspoon salt**

⅓   **cup mayonnaise**

3   **tablespoons milk**

¼   **cup sour cream**

3   **celery stalks, chopped**

¼   **cup chives, chopped**

Cut larger potatoes into 1 inch pieces. Place potatoes into large saucepan filled with enough water to cover them. Bring to boil, lower heat and simmer approximately 10 minutes until potatoes are fork tender.

Grate 1 teaspoon lemon zest and squeeze ½ cup juice from lemon in a large bowl. Whisk together lemon juice, lemon zest, oil, sugar and salt.

Drain potatoes and add hot potatoes to lemon mixture to coat. Let mixture cool. In another bowl, mix mayonnaise, milk and sour cream. When potatoes have cooled to room temperature, add mayonnaise mixture, celery and chives. Refrigerate until chilled.

Shared by Tammy Williams

This salad is a family favorite! I've been making it for years. It is especially tasty when cooking out in the summer.

COMPOTE SALAD WITH GRILLED CHICKEN, FRUIT, NUTS AND ROQUEFORT CHEESE

Wash, dry and remove all fat and membranes from chicken. Coat chicken with 2 tablespoons olive oil and generously cover with salt and pepper. Grill on both sides until meat is cooked and shows grill marks. Wash, dry and cut or tear romaine into bite size pieces. Core tomatoes and apple slices into ¼-inch wedges, put apple slices in bowl with lemonade and coat well to preserve color. Dry apples on paper towel. In a small bowl, whisk together ½ cup olive oil, balsamic vinegar, garlic, half teaspoon salt and pepper. Place aside. Cover large round platter with romaine pieces, fan the tomato slices around the outer edge of platter, fan cucumber slices inside the tomato slices. Make concentric rings of olive, apple and nuts. Pile cheese in the center of platter. Carefully cut chicken breast diagonally into ¼-inch thick slices, put slices back together in the shape. Arrange the chicken atop the salad in the 4 directions with the tips pointing toward the center. Whisk the dressing and drizzle over the salad. Serve promptly.

Add a crusty bread for a wonderful lunch or light summer dinner.

Shared by Holly Algood

4	small boneless chicken breast halves
2	small heads romaine lettuce
2	large tomatoes
1	granny smith apple
½	cup Calamata olives, pitted
⅓	cup walnut or pecan halves
½	English cucumber, thinly sliced
⅓	cup roquefort cheese, crumbled
½	cup cold lemonade
½	cup balsamic vinegar
½	cup plus 2 tablespoons virgin olive oil
1	garlic clove, pressed fine
salt	and white pepper, to taste

SEARED SHRIMP SALAD WITH LEMON PEPPER VINAIGRETT

Salad:

1 **cup lemon pepper vinaigrette**

16 **large shrimp, peeled and deveined**

1 **teaspoon Creole seasoning**

4 **cups arugula and bibb lettuce**

16 **spears large asparagus, peeled and blanched quickly**

Lemon pepper vinaigrette

1 **large egg**

2 **tablespoons fresh squeezed lemon juice**

2 **tablespoons fresh parsley, chopped**

1 **tablespoon Dijon mustard**

½ **teaspoon salt**

¾ **cup good olive oil**

salt and pepper, to taste

Toss the shrimp in a bowl with the creole seasoning. Heat a large dry skillet over high heat. When the skillet is hot, add the shrimp and sear them quickly for 3 minutes per side.

Lemon Pepper Vinaigrette:

Combine egg, lemon juice, parsley, mustard and salt in a food processor. Slowly add the olive oil.

To serve salad:

Mound the lettuce on each plate, fan 4 asparagus spears from the center of each plate, place shrimp in between each asparagus spear and drizzle the dressing over the shrimp.

Shared by Jen Carroll

This is a wonderful, unusual combination for a salad. The only way to make it is by using very fresh shrimp and asparagus. It can be served as a dinner entree with fresh bread on a warm summer evening.

The term wedding soup refers to a traditional menu item served at Italian weddings, but also to the blending or "marriage" of meats and vegetables. There are many variations to this recipe. Some recipes use escarole or broccoli florets, celery and carrots. Others use Italian sausage and salami as well as ground beef, veal or pork. My mother, who was born and raised in Calabria, served this soup at holiday family gatherings. According to her telling of folk lore, the main ingredients represent an aspect of marriage: meatballs — the blending of different families; the sharp-tasting greens—the bitterness or hard times of marriage; sugar, the good times and joy; pastina stands for the children.

ZUPPA MARITATA- WEDDING SOUP

Meatballs:

½ pound ground beef

½ pound ground veal, pork or turkey (my mother used veal only)

¼ cup bread crumbs (packaged or crusty Italian bread)

1 egg

1 tablespoon parsley, finely chopped

½ clove garlic, minced

½ teaspoon paprika

½ teaspoon salt and pepper, to taste

a pinch of sugar (my mother's addition)

Combine the ground meats, bread crumbs, egg, parsley, minced garlic and salt, pepper and sugar in mixing bowl. Mix well with a fork and form into tiny meatballs (about the size of a golf ball). Place meatballs on a greased baking sheet and bake for about 25 minutes at 350°, until brown; or you can sauté the meatballs in olive oil until brown. About 10 minutes before serving, bring the chicken broth to a boil, add the spinach and cook until tender. Add the meatballs and return soup to a simmer. Stir in the romano cheese and serve.

Shared by RoseMarie Tamburri

For the soup:

4 cups chicken broth

2 cups spinach, chopped

¼ cup grated Romano cheese

OPTIONAL: Orzo - small grains of pasta shaped like barley. (My mother also used pastina instead of orzo.)

GRILLED VEGETABLE SALAD

⅓ cup white balsamic vinegar

2 tablespoons olive oil

2 shallots, finely chopped

1 teaspoon dried Italian seasoning

salt and pepper, to taste

1½ teaspoons molasses

½ pound carrots, scraped, cut in pieces

1 red pepper, seeded, cut in pieces

1 yellow pepper, seeded, cut in pieces

2 zucchini, sliced into pieces

2 yellow squash, sliced into pieces

1 onion, cut in pieces

Combine first six ingredients in large bowl. Add chopped vegetables and toss. Let marinate for at least 30 minutes, stirring occasionally.

Remove veggies from mixture. Save vinegar mixture. Arrange veggies in grill basket and grill over medium to hot temperature with grill lid down for about 15-20 minutes, turning 2-3 times.

When veggies are done, toss with reserved vinegar mixture and serve warm. You can also cover and refrigerate overnight. Great the next day for topping a green salad.

Shared by Cindi Gardner

This is a great salad anytime, but especially in the summer when you can go to the vegetable stands and pick up home-grown vegetables. I have served this as a side dish, or tossed this with pasta. The flavor is great and even better the next day!

Grilled Vegetable Salad

SUMMER TOMATO STACK

Yellow tomatoes
Red tomatoes
Fresh basil leaves
   whole
Fresh large balls of
   mozzarella
balsamic vinaigrette

Slice tomatoes and cheese. Stack one yellow tomato, cheese, one red tomato, cheese, and basil leaf. Make a plate of these tomato cheese stacks and drizzle your favorite dressing over them. Season with salt and pepper and serve with warm crusty bread. Make sure you toss a few extra basil leaves onto your platter!

BARBARA'S FLANK STEAK MARINADE

¾   cup vegetable oil
¼   cup wine vinegar
½   tablespoon coarse
     ground pepper
⅛   cup Worcestershire
     sauce
¼   cup soy sauce
1   teaspoon dry
     mustard
1   clove garlic, crushed
1⅛ teaspoon salt
¾   teaspoon fresh parsley,
     chopped

Mix all of the ingredients together. Pour over steak and marinate for 5-6 hours.

Grill steak to desired doneness. Brush remaining marinade on meat as it cooks.

Shared by Barbara Gibbons

This marinade was given to me by a friend over 25 years ago. It's wonderful and can be used on any type of beef. I often use it on sirloin steak. It is also delicious with flank steak.

Summer Tomato Stack

MUSTARD SAUCE FOR TOMATOES

1   glove garlic, minced

1   teaspoon sugar

2   teaspoons prepared
    mustard

¼   cup salad oil

2   tablespoons tarragon
    vinegar

salt and pepper, to taste

This recipe is so easy and delicious. It makes a beautiful presentation on a rectangular platter with the different flavors and colors. Great alternative to a salad or side dish.

Combine all ingredients, and make sure they are well blended. Pour over freshly sliced tomatoes. Sprinkle with parsley and serve. Alternative–arrange slices of avocado and sliced tomatoes on plate and drizzle mustard sauce over for a wonderful, light salad.

Shared by Susan Miller

RASPBERRY VINAIGRETTE DRESSING AND SALAD

½   cup sugar

½   small onion, chopped

1   cup vegetable oil

2   teaspoons raspberry jam

½   cup raspberry vinegar

1   teaspoon salt

½   teaspoon dry mustard

Pureé sugar and onion in blender until it looks smooth. Slowly add oil, raspberry jam, vinegar, salt and mustard. Refrigerate and shake well.

For salad, mix bibb lettuce and red leaf lettuce, toasted walnut pieces, blue cheese, red grapes, sliced in halves. Arrange on individual salad plates and drizzle with raspberry vinaigrette.

BEET AND GRAPEFRUIT SALAD

On a hot and humid summer evening, when no one feels like eating dinner, I am often searching for something light and nutritious to serve. This salad is perfect, the beets are cool, refreshing and light. I often add some grilled. The salad is also wonderful for lunch served with a nice glass of chilled Pinot Grigio!

Cook beets in boiling water until tender, approximately 20 minutes. Remove from water and cool completely. Remove skins from beets and grate coarsely in a small bowl. Pour 4 tablespoons olive oil and vinegar over beets. Set aside. In a small skillet, heat 2 tablespoons butter. Roll goat cheese balls in bread crumbs, lightly fry goat cheese balls in butter, being careful not to burn.

Mound 4 salad plates with both types of lettuce. Spoon beet mixture on one side of each plate. Alternate grapefruit sections and goat cheese balls on other side of plate. Drizzle salad with remaining 4 teaspoons olive oil. Season to taste with salt and pepper.

Shared by Phyllis Carroll

4   fresh beets

8   teaspoons extra virgin olive oil

2   tablespoons balsamic vinegar

1   cup Romaine lettuce, shredded

1   cup bibb lettuce, shredded

2   grapefruits, peeled, pits removed and sectioned

2   ounces goat cheese, chilled and rolled into 8 small, round balls

2   tablespoons butter

½   cup bread crumbs

salt and pepper, to taste

DUNGENESS CRAB CEVICHE

4   pounds Dungeness
    crab, cooked
3   limes, juiced
1   avocado, chopped
1   bunch of cilantro,
    chopped

Pick crabmeat. Mix crabmeat with the juice of the limes.
Gently stir in avocado and cilantro to taste. Allow 1 hour
for flavors to absorb.

Serve over a bed of lettuce for a nice cool summer salad.
Serve with crackers as an appetizer. Serve in a wrap for a
delicious sandwich.

Shared by Diane Stone

*After having Ceviche at a
wonderful restaurant in
Vermont, I thought this
could be the answer at home
I have served this many
times now at different
occasions and found that
everyone loved the
refreshing flavors together.*

*This is a great do-ahead summer dish and only
gets better after an overnight
in the fridge.*

OODLES O' NOODLES-TANGLEWOOD SALAD

Cook chicken in water or broth; let cool and tear into bite sized pieces. Cover and put in fridge. Cook noodles in 4 quarts boiling water until very al dente. Drain and toss in a large bowl (preferably glass or ceramic) with ½-cup soy sauce, then peanut oil. Cool to room temperature, stirring occasionally to coat the noodles thoroughly.

Combine mayonnaise with mustard, sesame oil, the remaining ¼-cup soy sauce, and chili oil to taste. Cover and refrigerate until you've chopped all the other stuff.

To the large bowl of noodles, add chicken pieces, green onions, carrots, sweet pepper, bamboo shoots, miniature corn and chopped cilantro. Mix gently, but thoroughly with your hands. Add the mayonnaise mixture and blend well, again hands are great. Cover bowl tightly and refrigerate until ready to serve, preferably overnight. Trim the snow peas, cut into julienne. Blanch until crisp-tender, then chill in ice water and drain. Reserve these in a zipper bag in fridge until ready to serve. About 30 minutes before serving, remove noodle mixture from fridge and toss in julienned snow peas, adding a little extra soy sauce and peanut oil or mayonnaise if the noodles seem dry. Garnish with cilantro sprigs. You can be generous with the chili oil; cold noodles can take a lot of "heat."

Shared by Shelley Farmer

2	whole boneless, skinless chicken breasts
1	pound thin "mein" noodles
¾	cup soy sauce
¼	cup peanut oil
2	cups mayonnaise
1	tablespoon Dijon mustard
¼	cup oriental style sesame oil
	Szechuan chili oil
1	8 ounce can drained sliced bamboo shoots
1	can miniature corn on the cob, drained and sliced
½	cup cilantro, chopped
½	pound fresh snow peas
6	green onions, thinly sliced
2	carrots, peeled and coarsely chopped
1	sweet red pepper, seeded and coarsely chopped

SZECHUAN CHICKEN SALAD

2	whole chicken breasts, boiled and shredded
1	tablespoon soy sauce
2	tablespoons hoisin sauce
1	tablespoon corn syrup, Karo
½	teaspoon red pepper flakes
¼	cup peanut oil, or whatever is available
¼	cup chopped scallions, green or white
2	teaspoons ginger, minced
2	cups bok choy or Chinese cabbage, sliced

In a small saucepan combine pepper flakes, oil, scallions and ginger. Bring to a boil and remove from heat. In a large mixing bowl, combine mixture with the soy sauce, corn syrup and hoisin sauce. Combine shredded chicken and sliced bok choy, mix again. Serve chilled.

Shared by Shelley Farmer

BROCCOLI SALAD

1	small onion, finely chopped
1½	cups Hellman's mayonnaise
6	tablespoons sugar
6	tablespoons white vinegar
3	cups white cheddar cheese
3	bunches broccoli, rinsed and trimmed into small florets
1½	pounds bacon

The day before serving, combine the first five ingredients in a bowl. Pour this over the broccoli florets and mix well. Cover tightly and refrigerate overnight. An hour or more before serving, cook bacon and drain well. Toss bacon into broccoli mixture and mix thoroughly before serving.

Shared by Shelley Farmer

JOE'S FISH STOCK

Boil head of salmon, (you can get it from a fish store), in 6 cups of water. Add 1 onion chopped in large pieces, 2 carrots, chopped in large pieces, handful of parsley, 6-7 whole peppercorns, 1 teaspoon salt, and 2 whole tomatoes from can. Simmer for 2 hours on low heat. Strain and reserve liquid.

Shared by Joe Coniglialo of Bradley and Wall

BOB'S FLANK STEAK MARINADE

Although my wife is generally the chef in the family, this is one of the recipes that I like to prepare, as it is always well received by family and friends!

Mix all ingredients together. Pour over flank steak and let marinate over night.

Shared by Bob Graham

3 tablespoons scallion, minced
1½ tablespoons soy sauce
2 tablespoons olive oil
½ teaspoon thyme
big pinch of pepper
3 drops Tabasco sauce
juice of half of lemon

VEGGIES, VEGGIES AND MORE VEGGIES

Corn Bread Pudding

Avita's Cuban Black Beans

Sautéed Carrots

Sautéed Cauliflower

Panacotte

Grilled Veggies

Dino's Broccoli Rabe

Sesame Noodles

Nanny's String Beans

Wasabi Mashed Potatoes

Tina's Easy Asparagus

Sandi's Potatoes

Cranberry Apple Casserole

Vegetable Pie

Yam, Potato and Carrot Casserole

EGGIES, VEGGIES AND MORE VEGGIES

CORN BREAD PUDDING

3   cups stale corn bread
3   eggs
1   pint half and half
1   tablespoon honey
1   teaspoon vanilla

Spray 3-quart casserole dish with Pam. Crumble corn bread and place into bottom of casserole. Mix remaining ingredients into casserole. Pour over corn bread, making sure all the bread is covered.

Bake at 350° for 45 minutes. The corn bread should be moist.

Shared by Sue Zaccagnino

This recipe is just really good. A wonderful accompaniment to any meat dish. This is real comfort food! Enjoy!

AVITA'S CUBAN BLACK BEANS

This recipe originates from my Puerto Rican grand-mother, Avita. Being a small child, I could not pronounce the word "abuelita", which means "grandmother" in Spanish. Thus, the name "Avita" was born. Avita, who lived in Havana, Cuba, during the early part of the 20th century, learned to make the best Cuban black beans I've ever tasted. She used to make them from "scratch", soaking the beans overnight and then boiling them prior to adding all the ingredients.

Heat olive oil in a saucepan and add garlic, onions, and bell peppers. Sauté until soft. Add the can of black beans and mix together over low heat. Add the cumin, sugar, vinegar, bay leaf, salt and black pepper and let simmer for 10 minutes, over low heat. Add chopped cilantro and drizzle extra virgin olive oil before serving. Serve over plain white rice.

Shared by Ine Reardon

3 tablespoons olive oil
2 cloves garlic, chopped
1 onion, diced
½ green bell pepper or cubanelle pepper, diced
1 16 ounce can of Goya black beans (not black bean soup)
1 teaspoon ground cumin
1 teaspoon sugar or sherry
1 teaspoon cider vinegar
1 dried bay leaf, whole
1 teaspoon black pepper
1½ tablespoons fresh cilantro, chopped
salt, to taste

SAUTÉED CARROTS

10 small whole carrots, with greens on
10 slices of prosciutto
3 cloves garlic, chopped
2 pinches of kosher salt
2 pinches of sugar
handful of fresh sage, chopped
olive oil for sautéing

Using large fry pan heat olive oil, and start to sauté garlic, add whole carrots, and sauté on low until carrots are slightly tender, sprinkle kosher salt and sugar, as you are shaking the fry pan. Remove carrots and wrap with prosciutto, return to very low heat and toss in sage. Cook for another 1-2 minutes and let carrots rest in pan to absorb all flavors. This makes a beautiful plated side dish with the greens of carrots. Serve with beef, pork or chicken.

SAUTÉED CAULIFLOWER

1 head cauliflower, cut into florets
3 eggs, beaten
⅓ cup grated parmesan cheese
¼ teaspoon salt
3 tablespoons olive oil

Mix eggs, cheese and salt. Heat olive oil in sauté pan, to medium heat. Dip florets into egg and cheese mixture. Saute floret until golden brown. Salt to taste. Serve hot!

Shared by Terri Ednie

Being Italian, I was raised on eating good tasting vegetables, this recipe being one my mother made. It is a hit in my family, my son, Patrick is always asking for more white broccoli.

Christmas Eve, spent every year with special family and friends, consists of serving seven fish dishes and several side dishes. One dish that we serve as a fish accompaniment on Christmas Eve in our home and for other special occasions is Panacotte.

PANACOTTE

Sauté garlic (whole) in olive oil. Remove pan from heat and remove garlic. Add red pepper and escarole. Begin cooking again for 15 minutes, until slightly wilted. Add beans with juice and bring to a boil. Season with salt and pepper.

Put bread cubes in a casserole dish and sprinkle with ¼ cup parmesan cheese. Place escarole and beans on top of bread cubes. Sprinkle with remaining cheese. Bake at 375° for 20 minutes.

Shared by Sue Zaccagnino

1	head of escarole, washed and torn into pieces
4	whole garlic cloves
2	tablespoons olive oil (or more!)
½	teaspoon crushed, red pepper flakes
1	16 ounce can cannellini beans with juice
2	cups cubed stale Italian bread
½	cup freshly grated parmesan cheese

salt and pepper, to taste

GRILLED VEGGIES

Use all your favorites, fresh from the garden.

yellow squash

zucchini

onion

eggplant

red pepper

yellow pepper

green pepper

mushrooms

asparagus

¼ cup olive oil

salt and pepper, to taste

Wash and slice your favorite veggies into long pieces, coat with olive oil and salt and pepper to taste. Grill over medium heat until tender.

This is a great side dish. Sprinkle the veggies with a little balsamic vinegar for a different flavor. Shred parmigiano reggiano cheese on veggies while on grill for another variation.

Grilled Veggies

DINO'S BROCCOLI RABE

1 bunch broccoli rabe, about 1 pound
10 garlic cloves, sliced
¼ cup olive oil
salt and pepper, to taste

Wash and clean broccoli rabe. Remove tough ends of stems. Blanch in boiling water until stems are soft. Remove from water and cool to stop cooking process.

Sauté slices of garlic in olive oil until golden brown, add broccoli rabe, and toss. Add salt and pepper, to taste.

Shared by Dino Landino of Balladino's

SESAME NOODLES

4 tablespoons sesame oil
½ cup teriyaki sauce
1 tablespoon honey
2 tablespoons soy sauce
2 cloves fresh garlic, crushed
1 tablespoon olive oil
2 teaspoons fresh ginger, minced
2 carrots, shredded
2 tablespoons sesame seeds
1 scallion, chopped
1 handful fresh cilantro
¼ cup cashews, crushed
½ red pepper, chopped
½ green pepper, chopped
1 pound thin spaghetti

Boil 1 pound spaghetti until cooked al dente, set aside and cool. Bake cashews for 5 minutes on 350°. In a small bowl combine cashews with sesame seeds, set aside. Mix teriyaki, honey, soy sauce, garlic, ginger, sesame oil, olive oil, peppers, carrots, scallions, and cilantro. Mix completely. Pour mixture over spaghetti and top with cashew and sesame seeds. Refrigerate and serve at room temperature, can be made one day ahead.

Shared by Liz Wallack

Dino's Broccoli Rabe

NANNY'S STRING BEANS

1½   pounds fresh string beans

5   cloves garlic, sliced thin

1   tablespoon basil, dried

½   cup olive oil

Wash strings beans and trim ends. Steam green beans until tender and bright green. Drain string beans and return to steaming pot, add garlic, basil and olive oil to coat beans. Cover and let flavors absorb into beans for at least 5 minutes. Serve warm as is or serve cold drizzled with balsamic vinegar.

Shared by Chris Rinere

I learned everything I know about cooking from my grandmother (Nanny). This simple recipe is the first of many that she taught me and I have since taught my daughters, who can make them to perfection on their own!

WASABI MASHED POTATOES

3   pounds russet potatoes, peeled, cut into 2-inch pieces

¾   cup whole or 2% milk

2   tablespoons wasabi powder or paste, depending on your taste

¼   cup butter (½ stick)

Place potatoes in large pot of cold salted water. Boil about 20 minutes until tender. Drain and return to pot and mash. Combine ¾ cup milk and wasabi in small bowl. Stir to mix, add butter and milk mixture to the potatoes. Beat potatoes with electric mixer until fluffy. Season with salt and pepper.

Shared by Kris Moss

Nanny's String Beans

TINA'S EASY ASPARAGUS

1 bunch asparagus
1 package Good
Season's Italian
Dressing Mix

Parboil asparagus for about 2 minutes, no longer, as these should be a little crispy. Drain and put in cold water to stop cooking. Mix dressing as per package instructions and put in ziploc bag with asparagus and shake. Refrigerate over night. Serve on a bed of greens at room temperature.

Shared by Tina Garrity

SANDI'S POTATO DISH

6 medium potatoes
¼ cup butter
2 cups cheddar cheese, shredded
2 cups sour cream
⅓ cup scallions, chopped
1 teaspoon salt
¼ teaspoon pepper
2 tablespoons butter

Cook potatoes in skins, then chill. Peel and grate potatoes in large bowl. Over low heat combine ¼ cup butter and cheese until almost melted. Remove from heat and blend in sour cream, scallions and seasonings. Pour cheese mixture over potatoes and stir to blend. Put into a greased casserole and dot with 2 tablespoons butter. Bake at 350° for 45 minutes.

Shared by Sandi McKinnon

CRANBERRY APPLE CASSEROLE

In a 1½ -quart casserole dish, mix apples and cranberries. Sprinkle white sugar over mixture. Melt butter in sauce pan. Mix oatmeal, flour and brown sugar and add to melted butter. Stir well. Sprinkle butter mixture over cran-apple mixture, covering it completely with butter and flour mixture. Bake at 1 hour for 350°. Then add nuts and bake for another 5-8 minutes.

Shared by Susan Miller

3	cups tart apples, unpeeled and cubed
2	cups cranberries
¾	cup sugar
1	stick butter or margarine
1	cup oatmeal
⅓	cup brown sugar
½	cup nuts, chopped
⅓	cup flour

VEGETABLE PIE

2   medium-sized zucchinis, cut into ⅛ inch slices
4   medium sized tomatoes, cut into half inch slices
1   tablespoon Dijon mustard
1   cup shredded, mozzarella cheese
1   Pillsbury pre-made pie crust (red box in refrigerator aisle)
2   teaspoons olive oil
½   teaspoon basil
½   teaspoon oregano
1   clove garlic, crushed
salt and pepper, to taste

Spray pie plate with cooking spray. Line pie crust in pie dish. Spread mustard all over bottom of pie crust. Sprinkle cheese all over mustard. Alternate tomato and zucchini slices, standing up in a fan like fashion working towards the middle from the outside of the pie plate. Drizzle olive oil over top and sprinkle seasonings. Bake at 375° for 45 minutes.

Shared by Kim Castaldo

YAM, POTATO AND CARROT CASSEROLE

1   tablespoon butter
¾   cup half and half
    dash freshly ground nutmeg
1   teaspoon salt
1   teaspoon pepper
1   pound russet potatoes
1   pound yams
1   pound carrots
⅓   cup chives, chopped
⅓   cup parmesan cheese

Butter 8 x 8 x 2 inch casserole dish. In a small bowl, combine half and half, salt, pepper and nutmeg. Peel potatoes, yams and carrots, slice all 3 into ¼-inch slices cover bottom of casserole with single layer of potatoes. Drizzle with cream mixture. Cover with single layer of yams. Drizzle with cream mixture cover with single layer of carrots. Drizzle with cream mixture. Repeat layering with 3 vegetables. Cover top layer with parmesan cheese. Bake for 45 minutes at 345°.

Vegetable Pie

PASTA AND SAUCES

Fettuccine Campagnola

Fettuccine Alfredo with Pancetta and Peas

Fast and Fabulous Tomato Sauce

Balladino's Fresh Marinara Sauce

Balladino's Tuscan Sauce

Summertime Italian Tomato Pasta

Gnocchi Sorrentinna

The Madison Bistro's Penne a la Vodka

Chicken Parmigiano over Linguini

Liz's Pink Vodka Sauce

Castaldo's Bolognaise Sauce

Linguini with Veggies and Basil

Fettuccine 4

Tom's Pasta with Chicken and Pink Vodka Sauce

Spaghetti Al Nero Di Seppie

Summer Vegetable Lasagna

Garlic Sherry Shrimp with Pasta

Paige and Nicole's Pasta Primavera

PASTAS AND SAUCES

FETTUCCINE CAMPAGNOLA

¾ **pound egg noodles**

6 **garlic cloves, chopped**

10 **asparagus spears, parboiled 2-3 minutes, chopped, discard about 1-inch from bottom of stem**

20 **Calamato olives, chopped**

1 **whole chicken breast grilled with fresh rosemary, sliced**

5 **tablespoons pesto sauce**

6 **tablespoons of boiling water from pasta**

parmigiano reggiano

Start with cold virgin olive oil, add garlic, asparagus, olives and chicken. Sauté on medium high heat, adding water from pasta. Sauté until garlic is golden. Water will evaporate. Cook about 1-2 minutes. Stir up bottom of sauté pan and mix for flavor. Meanwhile, cook egg noodles, al dente. Place noodles in middle of chicken and with tongs, gently mix. Next, add pesto sauce and toss. Never cook pesto sauce. Transfer to individual serving bowls and sprinkle with freshly grated parmigiano reggiano. Serve immediately. This is a farmers-style dish, from Italy, using all fresh, natural ingredients.

Shared by Andrea Panno of The Madison Bistro

FETTUCCINE ALFREDO WITH PANCETTA AND PEAS

Melt butter in sauce pan, and add heavy cream and cheese to melted butter. Whisk over medium heat until sauce thickens. Turn off heat and add parsley, frozen peas, and pancetta. Cook for 1 minute, just long enough to cook peas. Toss with pasta, and serve with shavings of fresh cheese and warm crusty bread!

1   pound pasta
1   stick butter
1½ cups heavy cream
1   cup parmigiano reggiano, freshly grated
½   cup flat leaf parsley, chopped
1   pound pancetta, cooked and diced
1   bag frozen peas

FAST AND FABULOUS TOMATO SAUCE

Cut up the plum tomatoes, with their juice, try to remove as many seeds as possible. Add to a large sauté pan with the onion and butter and salt. Simmer slowly (uncovered) for about 45 minutes stirring and mashing tomatoes with the back of a wooden spoon from time to time. Taste and add salt if necessary. Discard onion before serving, serve over your favorite pasta and add cheese if desired. This recipe is soooooooooo fast and easy.......kids love it!

2   cups imported Italian plum tomatoes
5   tablespoons butter
1   medium to large onion, peeled and cut in half
kosher or sea salt, to taste
1   pound pasta, cooked al dente
freshly grated parmesan cheese

Shared by Faith Whitehead

BALLADINO'S FRESH MARINARA SAUCE

1   29 ounce can whole
    plum tomatoes
10 garlic cloves, chopped
salt and pepper, to taste
8   fresh basil leaves,
    torn
olive oil extra virgin, use
    good olive oil

Sauté garlic in extra virgin olive oil until golden brown. Take can of whole tomatoes, crush with your hands, and add to garlic. Add salt and pepper, to taste. Add torn basil leaves and simmer on low for about 20 minutes.

Shared by Dino Landino of Balladino's

This recipes originates from Southern Italy. If you double the recipe, add about 5 extra minutes for simmering.

BALLADINO'S TUSCAN SAUCE

3   carrots, coarsely
    chopped
3   celery, coarsely chopped
1   large onion, coarsely
    chopped
8   garlic cloves, chopped
1   20 ounce can plum
    tomatoes (I like
    San Marzano)
8   fresh basil leaves, torn
olive oil for sautéing and
    extra to thin out sauce
water, as needed to thin
    sauce
1   pound pasta, cooked
    al dente

Sauté the carrots, celery, onion, and garlic until almost caramelized, golden brown. Crush plum tomatoes with hands, and add to sauté mixture. Cook 10-15 minutes. Puree sauce, and return to sauce pan. Add fresh basil, salt and pepper, to taste. Sauce is very thick, thin to proper consistency with a little olive oil and water. Toss with freshly cooked pasta. My favorite is Liuzzi.

Shared by Dino Landino of Balladino's

SUMMERTIME ITALIAN TOMATO PASTA

Peel tomatoes, coarsely chop over a bowl. Reserve juice. Combine tomatoes, juice, olive oil. Add garlic, basil, salt, pepper, olives and parsley. Let stand at room temperature for at least 1 hour. Cook pasta and drain. Serve tomato mixture over pasta. Top with good Italian grating cheese.

This recipe can be doubled for a crowd. I make it all the time! Serve with Italian bread, and a spinach salad and nice glass of wine.

Shared by Audrey Weber

3   large vine-ripened tomatoes
3   cloves garlic, minced
1   tablespoon fresh basil
¼   teaspoon salt
¼   teaspoon pepper
¼   cup ripe olives
2   tablespoons fresh parsley, chopped
4   ounces spaghetti
4   ounce mozzarella cheese, cut into cubes
2   tablespoons extra virgin olive oil.

GNOCCHI SORRENTINA

2 cups home-made red sauce
1 pound gnocchi pasta
½ cup parmesan cheese, grated
¼ pound whole milk mozzarella, cut into ¼ inch cubes
1 bunch fresh basil, chopped

Cook gnocchi according to directions on package. In a heavy skillet, warm red sauce over medium heat. Drain cooked gnocchi and return to pot. Pour red sauce, parmesan cheese and mozzarella cheese over gnocchi. Toss until pasta is well coated and the mozzarella begins to soften. Sprinkle with basil and serve warm.

Shared by Chef Silvio of Cafe Allegre

THE MADISON BISTRO'S   PENNE A LA VODKA

4 tablespoons red onion, finely chopped
extra virgin olive oil
1 shot of vodka
2½ cups marinara sauce
½ cup heavy cream
3 tablespoons butter
¼ cup parmigiano reggiano, finely grated
1 pound penne pasta, cooked

Put onion into cold olive oil and sauté, when you hear the sizzle of onions, add vodka and flame, about 5 seconds. Add marinara sauce and sauté for about 20 seconds until sauce starts to boil, continue to stir the whole time, add ½ cup of heavy cream and butter, mix well and add cheese. Cook 2 minutes and toss with hot pasta. Top with shaving of parmigiano reggiano and serve.

Shared by Andrea Panno of The Madison Bistro

Gnocchi Sorrentina

Growing up in an Italian/Irish family inspires many traditions, involving a love of great food and a desire to share it with those we cherish. Since most of our family members are women (we have over twenty aunts), this meant lots of cooks and endless recipes. Also, there was never a shortage of special occasions and holidays between these two cultures, especially at Christmas and Easter time. So, many happy meals were savored by all of the fathers, uncles, cousins, nieces and nephews, in-laws and friends who joined our table over the years. Some of these wonderful people are gone now, many are still here, and still more join us. Amazingly, we truly enjoy each other's company and look forward to the opportunities to celebrate any event.

CHICKEN PARMIGIANO WITH LINGUINE

3   pounds of chicken breast, trimmed and sliced thin

2½ cups seasoned bread crumbs

1   cup fresh parmesan cheese

1   pound fresh mozzarella cheese, sliced thin or grated

6   tablespoons olive oil

2   raw eggs, beaten with ¼ cup milk

2   cups warm Italian style marinara sauce

salt and pepper, to taste

1   pound pasta, cooked al dente

Preheat oven to 350°. In a medium to large skillet, heat oil. Place beaten eggs in a bowl. Place bread crumbs and ½ cup of parmesan cheese in a flat plate. Dip each cutlet into the egg mixture and then thoroughly coat each cutlet in the bread crumbs. Timesaver, bread these early in the morning, refrigerate and cook later. Place ½ cup of warmed sauce in baking dish. Fry the breaded cutlets in the oil until golden brown. Drain on paper towels. Arrange the cutlets in baking pan. Spread mozzarella cheese, the rest of the parmesan cheese and some salt and pepper over the cutlets. Top with more sauce and cook in the oven until the cheese melts, but do not burn, about 15 minutes. Serve immediately. These taste great the next day on heated Italian bread. Always keep extra sauce around for dipping with bread or topping off chicken. These cutlets freeze very well!

With love, Marion Ziccardi Malafronte, Susan Ziccardi Devany and Juliana Ziccardi

Chicken Parmigiano

LIZ'S PINK VODKA SAUCE

3 tablespoons olive oil

1 shallot

⅓ pound pancetta, finely chopped

1 16 ounce can Progresso crushed tomatoes with added puree

fresh basil, chopped, one handful

3 pinches of crushed red pepper

¼ cup vodka

fresh parmesan, grated

heavy cream

Coat pan with olive oil, add chopped shallot and pancetta, sauté 5 minutes, add can of tomatoes and chopped basil, sprinkle crushed red pepper, and simmer over low heat for about 10 minutes. Set heat to high, and add vodka, simmer 3-4 minutes, add heavy cream until light pink. Sprinkle with fresh parmesan cheese. Cook pasta of choice, while hot, sprinkle with cheese and chopped basil. Pour sauce over pasta, toss and serve.

Shared by Liz Wallack

CASTALDO'S BOLOGNAISE SAUCE

1 pound top sirloin beef, minced

1 large onion, chopped

6 strips bacon, cooked, drained and chopped

2 large cloves of garlic, finely chopped

1 8 ounce glass of good Cabernet

1 teaspoon dried oregano

1 teaspoon kosher salt

1 16 ounce can of diced tomatoes

1 6 ounce can tomato puree

black pepper, to taste

1 tablespoon olive oil

1 large handful fresh basil

1 small handful fresh Italian parsley

In a large frying pan warm 1 tablespoon of olive oil. Add beef, onion and garlic, cook over medium heat. Stir in wine, reduce until liquid is just about cooked off. Add oregano, tomatoes, and tomato puree and cooked bacon, salt and pepper, to taste. Bring to boil and reduce heat and simmer for about 90 minutes. Spoon over fresh linguine and cover with shredded basil and Italian parsley.

Shared by Kim Castaldo

LINGUINI WITH VEGGIES AND BASIL

Heat olive oil in large heavy skillet and add both types of onions. Cook until browned and soft, stir in the tomatoes and artichokes, add balsamic vinegar. Add cooked pasta and top with salt, pepper, basil and cheese. Serve warm.

1   pound linguine
1   Vidalia onion, peeled and chopped fine
1   red onion, peeled and chopped fine
4   tablespoons olive oil
1   cup sundried tomatoes in oil, drained and chopped
1   cup marinated artichokes in oil, drained and chopped
3   tablespoons balsamic vinegar
salt and pepper, to taste
1   bunch fresh basil, chopped
¼   cup parmesan cheese

FETTUCCINE 4

Cook pasta in boiling, salted water until al dente. Combine cream, three cheeses, butter, red pepper and nutmeg in a heavy large saucepan. Whisk over medium heat until mixture thickens and becomes smooth. Drain pasta and return to same pot. Add cream sauce and parmesan. Toss to coat and season with salt and pepper, to taste. Sprinkle with pine nuts and serve hot.

1   pound spinach fettuccine
1½ cups whipping cream
¾   cup gorgonzola cheese, crumbled
⅔   cup provolone cheese, grated
½   cup soft fresh goat cheese, crumbled
¼   cup butter
½   teaspoon red pepper, dried and crushed
¼   teaspoon ground nutmeg
¾   cup fresh parmesan cheese, grated
¼   cup pine nuts, toasted

TOM'S PASTA WITH CHICKEN AND PINK VODKA SAUCE

1½ pounds chicken breast, boneless, skinless
6 teaspoons olive oil
¾ teaspoon salt
3 cloves garlic, chopped
4 ounces vodka
1 quart jar prepared spaghetti sauce
4 ounces half and half (or sour cream)
12 ounces linguine, cooked to package directions
parmesan cheese, grated
salt and pepper, to taste

Cut chicken into pieces and salt. Heat oil in pan and sauté garlic over medium high heat. Reduce heat to medium and add chicken and mix with garlic while cooking. When chicken is lightly browned on both sides, add vodka and stir, let liquid reduce for a few minutes and stir in spaghetti sauce. Cover and simmer for 1-2 minutes. Stir in half and half, and cover again. Prepare linguine according to package instructions. Pour sauce over linguine and add salt and pepper, to taste. Top with freshly grated parmesan cheese.

Shared by Tom Banish

SPAGHETTI AL NERO DI SEPPIE (SPAGHETTI WITH SQUID)

2 tablespoons olive oil
3 small seppies, squid
2 shallots, chopped
4 cups tomato sauce
1 pound spaghetti, cooked al dente

Remove sacks with ink and juice from seppie, and reserve. Slice seppies into little pieces, set aside. Cover bottom of pan with oil and sauté chopped shallots until golden brown. Drop seppies into oil and slightly cook. Add tomato sauce in seppie pan and start to simmer. Open ink sacks, and add sacks and reserved juice to sauce. Cook for 15 minutes. Meanwhile, cook spaghetti and pour sauce over spaghetti. Serve immediately.

Shared by Andrea Panno of The Madison Bistro

SUMMER VEGETABLE LASAGNA

In the bottom of a 9 x 13 baking dish, layer the thinly sliced zucchini evenly across pan. Cover with ⅓ of the sharp cheese and ⅓ of the parmesan cheese, sprinkle with garlic salt. Place three lasagna noodles evenly across zucchini and cheese layer. Mix the onions, green pepper and garlic together and place evenly over lasagna noodles. Repeat with the layer of cheese and zucchini, followed by last three lasagna noodles. Layer the sliced tomatoes, pour the juice from the tomatoes evenly over the top. Place remaining cheeses on top of tomatoes. Bake at 350° for one hour or until top is golden brown. Let sit for 10-15 minutes before cutting into serving pieces. Note: use a 3mm Cuisinart slicing blade to slice the zucchini, onions, green pepper and tomatoes. This is an awesome recipe with fresh summer vegetables.

Shared by Barbara Gibbons

2	medium zucchini squash, sliced thin
1	large onion, sliced thin
1	medium green pepper, sliced thin
3	cloves of garlic, crushed
8	tomatoes, sliced thin
4	cups sharp cheese, shredded
1	cup fresh parmesan cheese
	garlic salt
6	no-bake lasagna noodles

GARLIC SHERRY SHRIMP WITH PASTA

5 tablespoons olive oil
4 garlic cloves, finely minced
1 teaspoon red pepper flakes
1 pound medium shrimp, peeled and deveined
¼ cup sherry
salt and pepper, to taste

In a large bowl, place all ingredients and toss together. Place ingredients into skillet and sauté over high heat until shrimp are done. Serve over linguini or with baguette pieces in a bowl.

Shared by Lisa Kronauer

Stop and Shop has bagged shrimp, that is easy to peel, in the specialty frozen section, and they work wonderful for this dish. Keep some shrimp in your freezer.

PAIGE AND NICOLE'S PASTA PRIMAVERA

¼ pound butter
2 garlic cloves, finely minced
¾ cup canned peas
¾ cup canned corn
¾ cup canned carrots
½ cup onion, chopped
2 tablespoons oregano
2 tablespoons basil
2 tablespoons parsley
1 pound spaghetti
salt and pepper, to taste

In a large skillet, over medium to high heat, melt butter. Add garlic, peas, corn and carrots and sauté until carrots are soft, approximately 5 minutes. Add onions, oregano, parsley and basil and sauté for another 2 minutes.

Cook pasta according to directions on box. Drain pasta and place in bowl. Salt and pepper. Mix together all ingredients and serve. You can sprinkle parmesan cheese on top, if desired.

Shared by Paige and Nicole Kronauer

My mom loves to cook this and we have so much fun helping her. The pasta we make we love to eat and it is so delicious, we hope you like it too!!

Garlic Sherry Shrimp with Pasta

POULTRY, PORK AND BEEF

Jeff's Apple Cider Osso Buco

Chicken In Wine

Apple Sweet Potato Beef Brisket

Mike B's "Pig Lickin Good" Baby Back Ribs

Filet of Beef with Bearnaise Sauce and Pan Roasted Tomatoes

Chicken Divan

"SNAKES"

Roast Pork Loin with Garlic And Rosemary

Lynette's Brisket

Veal Rack Allegre

Coq au Vin

Lauren's Chicken Dijon

Chicken Geno

Quick Italian Ham Pie

Best Chicken I've Ever Had

All-in-One-Chicken-Dish

Tina's Chicken

Japanese Ribs

Beef Burgundy

Hearty Hamburger Casserole

Mishe Me Preshe (Lamb with Leek Stew)

POULTRY PORK AND BEEF

JEFF'S APPLE CIDER OSSO BUCO

4   veal shanks
3   leeks
2   cups apple cider
1   can chicken stock
1   onion, chopped
2   cloves garlic, chopped
1   shallot, chopped
salt and pepper, to taste
1   tablespoon butter
1   tablespoon olive oil
flour, Wondra
3   tablespoons fresh
    tarragon, chopped

Tie the shanks with cooking twine so that they stay in one piece, or cook them as they are and break the meat off the bone as you toss them into the sauce. Use only the white portions of the leeks. Make several long slits into each leek and run them under cold water to rid them of sand. Slice up the leeks and combine with chopped onions, garlic and shallot in a sauté pan. Sauté over medium-high heat with a little water and a touch of salt for about 5 minutes. Set aside.

In a heavy ovenproof pot, melt butter and oil over a medium-high heat. Flour shanks and add to the pot, 1 or 2 at a time. Brown all sides and do not crowd while browning. Fit all 4 browned shanks into the bottom of pot. Add the cider, chicken stock and sautéed leeks, onions, garlic and shallot. Add the tarragon and a pinch of salt and pepper. Leeks should be completely covered with liquid. If not, add more cider. Cover and simmer for 30 minutes, and then bake in oven for 2 hours at 350 °. Remove from oven, place shanks on platter and cover with foil.

Drain liquid through a fine strainer into a mixing bowl, then put liquid back into pot. Discard vegetables. Boil liquid over high heat, until reduced to half. Reduce heat and thicken with flour. Break the meat off the bone and quickly toss in the sauce before serving. Serve hot.

Shared by Jeff Thornbury

This dish goes great with mashed potatoes and peas. A real hearty meal for those cold Connecticut nights! Enjoy!

Jeff's Apple Cider Osso Bucco

CHICKEN IN WINE

10 chicken breasts, halved
1 stick butter
2 cans cream of mushroom soup
½ soup can water
¾ cup sherry
1 large pack fresh mushrooms, sautéed (or large can of mushrooms)
salt and pepper, to taste

Salt and pepper chicken breasts. Brown chicken in butter in heavy skillet. Remove chicken from skillet and add soup, water, sherry and mushrooms to remaining butter. Cook over low heat for 5 minutes, stirring. Place chicken breasts in shallow dish, pour sauce over and bake for 1 hour at 350°. Serves 10

Shared by Lisa Carr

APPLE SWEET POTATO BEEF BRISKET

1 beef brisket, 5-6 pounds
2 medium onions, thinly sliced
¾ cup apple cider vinegar
1½ cups apple juice
1½ cups white wine
½ cup firmly packed brown sugar or maple syrup
salt and pepper, to taste
8 medium sweet potatoes (or regular potatoes)
3 cups carrots

Trim and discard excess fat from brisket. Put some of the onions and carrots in with the beef. Salt and pepper the meat, and add everything but the sweet potatoes, and bulk of onions and carrots.

Bake at 300° for about 2½ hours to 3 hours, and keep adding more apple juice/wine if the liquid evaporates. The last 1 to 1½ hours, add the rest of the veggies and cook until brisket is very tender, and the veggies are done. Cook for about a total of 4 hours.

Shared by Carmen Jane Booth

MIKE B'S "PIG LICKIN GOOD" BABY BACK RIBS

Mix all dry ingredients together. Rub dry mixture liberally onto both sides of each slab of ribs. Wrap each slab tightly with aluminum foil. Place wrapped ribs in refrigerator for at least 2 hours to chill (preferably overnight). Fill 2 cookie sheets with apple cider. Add 1 teaspoon liquid smoke to each cookie sheet. Place 2 foil wrapped slabs on each cookie sheet and bake for 1½ hours on 275°. Remove ribs from oven and foil. Coat each side with your favorite barbecue sauce. Broil or grill on barbecue for 5 minutes per side so that sauce can cook in.

This recipe was inspired by my many trips to Memphis on Pfizer business. In my opinion, Memphis is the world capital of BBQ and this recipe is intended to produce "Memphis Style" ribs without utilizing a traditional smoker. Enjoy!

Shared by Mike Barrella

4	slabs baby back ribs
3	tablespoons sugar
1	tablespoon black pepper
1	tablespoon mustard powder
2	tablespoons paprika
2	tablespoons kosher salt
2	tablespoons brown sugar
1	tablespoon cumin
2	teaspoons chili powder
1	tablespoon onion powder
1	tablespoon garlic powder
1	quart apple cider
	liquid smoke

FILET OF BEEF WITH BÉARNAISE SAUCE AND PAN ROASTED TOMATOES

2   filet of beef steaks,
     thick cut
kosher salt
freshly ground pepper
olive oil
Béarnaise (Star Fish Market
     in Guilford has a great
     Béarnaise sauce)
Grape tomatoes

Rub steaks with a little olive oil and press with salt and pepper. Grill on high heat for about 2 minutes on each side. Let rest. Prepare Béarnaise sauce as instructed on package and top the filets. Put grape tomatoes in hot sauté pan over high heat and cook for about 2 minutes, shaking pan continuously. Use about 6-8 grape tomatoes per person. Prepare plate and garnish with fresh sprigs of sage or rosemary.

Shared by Diane Gardner

CHICKEN DIVAN

1   baking chicken,
     roasted in oven
6   fresh broccoli crowns
     (broken into florets)
2   cups sharp cheddar
     cheese, shredded
2   cups milk
2   tablespoons butter
2   tablespoons flour
salt and pepper, to taste
parmesan cheese

Pull chicken off bone and cut into small pieces. Steam broccoli florets (just until they turn bright green), but still crunchy and then drain. Melt butter in sauce pan. Add flour, salt and pepper. Stir to form a paste. Add milk slowly and bring to boil. Continue cooking until it thickens, about 3-4 minutes. Add cheese to milk mixture, stir until all cheese is melted. In 9x13 baking dish, place broccoli on bottom of pan, spreading evenly across pan. Sprinkle broccoli with parmesan cheese. Place chicken pieces evenly over broccoli. Sprinkle chicken with parmesan cheese. Pour cheese sauce over chicken. Bake at 350° for 30 minutes, or until casserole is bubbly all over.

Shared by Barbara Gibbons

Filet of Beef with Béarnaise Sauce and Pan Roasted Tomatoes

The Roetting Children

Jaime,

Heidi,

Michelle

and Danielle

1977

This recipe has been a favorite family recipe for over 30 years, only served on special occasions. Our first born, Jaime, tantalized his three sisters, Heidi, Michelle, and Danielle with his forging into the woods, collecting specimens, his trophies frequently being tree frogs and oftentimes snakes.

"SNAKES"

Having served flank steak, cut on the bias into strips, marinated overnight, then grilled for our dinner, our Danielle, at 3 years old, took one look and declared she would NOT eat "snakes"!

The laughter around our dinner table established our family tradition.

Mix all the ingredients together in a large bowl. Add steak strips and coat. Refrigerate overnight. Grill 3-4 minutes. Enjoy!

Shared by Vilma Roetting Cook

1	flank steak, cut on the bias, ¾ inch thick, set aside
½	cup vegetable oil
1	cup catsup
1	clove garlic, crushed
2	tablespoons minced dried onions
2	tablespoons Tabasco sauce
2	tablespoons soy sauce
¾	teaspoons sugar

ROAST PORK LOIN WITH GARLIC AND ROSEMARY

4   **large garlic cloves, minced**

4   **teaspoons fresh rosemary, chopped**

1½ **teaspoons salt**

½   **teaspoon ground black pepper**

1   **pork loin roast, approximately 2 pounds, well trimmed**

fresh rosemary sprigs

1   **cup chicken stock**

¼   **cup white wine**

2   **tablespoons butter**

Line 13 x 9 x 2-inch roasting pan with tin foil. Mix first four ingredients in a bowl. Rub garlic mixture all over pork. Place pork, fat side down, in prepared roasting pan. Roast pork for 30 minutes on 400°. Turn roast to fat side up and roast until thermometer inserted into center of pork registers 155° (approximately 25 minutes longer). Add ½ cup chicken stock while roasting. Remove roast from oven and let stand for 10 minutes. Pour any juices from roasting pan into a small saucepan. Heat juices on low heat to keep warm. Add ½ cup chicken stock, white wine and butter to juices. Mix thoroughly over low heat. Cut pork crosswise into 1/3 inch thick slices. Arrange pork slices on platter and pour warm juices over pork. Garnish with rosemary sprigs.

Shared by Dani Woods

LYNETTE'S BRISKET

This is my mother's brisket recipe that my sisters and I make in her honor for all of our family holidays. The brisket is best when made the night before and reheated in the sauce. Enjoy!

Remove brisket from packaging and rinse with cold water. Pat brisket dry and place in disposable aluminum roaster. Cover the side facing up with 2 packets soup mix. Roast brisket for 20 minutes on 500°. Remove from oven, turn to other side and coat with remaining 2 packets soup mix. Roast for 20 minutes on 500°. Remove from oven and turn temperature down to 300°. Pour 6 cans red sauce over brisket. Fill empty sauce cans with water and pour over brisket. Brisket should be completely covered with liquid. Cover tightly with aluminum foil and place back in oven. Let brisket cook slowly for 3-4 hours or until brisket starts to fall apart.

Shared by Jill Swimmer

1	beef brisket, 3-5 pounds
4	packets Lipton onion soup mix
6	cans Arturo's red sauce
6	cans of water

VEAL RACK ALLEGRE

2 veal racks, frenched

½ cup porcine mushrooms (dried, presoaked or fresh)

1 tablespoon shallot, minced

2 ounces butter

½ cup demi glaze (or good brown gravy)

1½ ounces cognac

4 ounces heavy cream

salt and pepper, to taste

Roast veal rack on high heat (450-500°) approximately 25-40 minutes, according to desired preference. In a 10 inch skillet, combine butter and shallots. Cook or medium heat until shallots caramelized. Pull pan from heat, add cognac and mushrooms and return to stove. Cook and stir frequently for another 5-10 minutes. Reduce heat to low and add demi glaze and heavy cream. Continue to stir for another 5 minutes. Add salt and pepper, to taste. Adjust consistency by adding cream or demi glaze

Shared by Chef Silvio of Cafe Allegre

LAUREN'S CHICKEN DIJON

6 boneless chicken breasts, washed and trimmed

¼ cup olive oil

2 garlic cloves, chopped

juice of one fresh lemon, plus 2 teaspoons

¼ cup cooking sherry, plus 2 teaspoons

3 tablespoons country Dijon mustard

¼ cup butter

3 cups cooked white rice

Prepare marinade by combining olive oil, garlic, lemon juice and sherry. Pat dry chicken breasts and cover with salt and pepper. Wrap in wax paper, flatten until thin with mallet. Put chicken breasts in marinade and let soak overnight in refrigerator. Remove chicken breasts from marinade. In a baking casserole, lay chicken flat and coat top side with Dijon mustard. Broil until golden brown. Remove from oven and turn each piece over and broil this side until golden brown. Meanwhile, in a small heavy skillet, brown butter, 2 teaspoons lemon juice and 2 teaspoons sherry, whisked together. Pour this sauce over chicken and serve promptly with rice. Serves 6. This is the very first dish I ever made for my husband after we were married. It continues to be one of his favorites today!

Shared by Lauren Geary

Veal Rack Allegre

COQ AU VIN

2½ pounds chicken pieces
2   tablespoons cooking oil
18 shallots
¼   cup burgundy wine
1   cup mushrooms, whole
1   cup carrots, sliced thin
1   cup small potatoes
2   cloves garlic, minced
½   teaspoon marjoram
½   teaspoon thyme
1   bay leaf
2   tablespoons parsley
2   tablespoons flour
2   tablespoons butter, softened
3   slices bacon, cooked and crumbled
2   cups hot, cooked noodles
salt and pepper, to taste

Remove skin from chicken pieces. In a large skillet, over medium heat, cook chicken in oil. Cook approximately 15 minutes until browned on all sides. Sprinkle with salt and pepper. In a large cook pot, add chicken, onions, shallots, potatoes, burgundy, mushrooms and carrots. Add garlic, marjoram, thyme, bay leaf and 1 tablespoon parsley. Bring to a boil, reduce heat and cover, simmering for about 40 minutes until chicken is no longer pink. In a bowl, mix together flour and butter to form a paste. Stir into burgundy mixture in the large pot. Sprinkle with cooked bacon and additional parsley. Serve over hot, cooked noodles.

Shared by Tina Edwards

CHICKEN GENO

4   chicken breasts with bone in, skin removed
½   cup olive oil
1   garlic glove, crushed
1   small yellow onion, chopped
1   small bunch basil, chopped
1   8 ounce can crushed tomatoes

Wash chicken breasts and pat dry. Pour olive oil in bottom of 9 x 13 pan. Place chicken in pan and cover with remaining ingredients. Bake uncovered for 1 hour at 350°. Serve over white rice.

Shared by Gene Calzetta

QUICK ITALIAN HAM PIE

I received this recipe from my mother-in-law, Yolanda Valla. She died in December 2002 and was a tremendous cook. She made this dish every Easter.

Beat eggs, add milk and beat, add flour and mix and then fold in all ingredients. Mix with spoon until all combined. Bake at 350° for 50-60 minutes until lightly brown on top. Cut into squares and serve either warm or at room temperature.

Shared by Barbara Valla

¾ cup of milk

1½ cups flour

10 beaten eggs

1 stick of diced pepperoni

2 thick slices of ham, diced

6 ounces sharp cheddar cheese, diced

6 ounces Munster cheese, diced

2½ teaspoons baking powder

well greased 8 x 10-inch casserole dish

BEST CHICKEN I EVER HAD

I received this from a former boss, who was an excellent cook. I have since made it for countless families. It's a hit! Enjoy!

Mix all ingredients and bake at 350° in casserole for 1½ hours covered and ½ hour uncovered.

Shared by Barbara Parker

1 box Uncle Ben's Wild Rice

1 10½ ounce can of cream of celery soup

1 small can water chestnuts, sliced and drained

1 16 ounce can French cut green beans, drained

1 cup mayonnaise

2 cups chicken broth

4 cups cooked chicken, diced

ALL-IN-ONE CHICKEN DISH

12 pieces of chicken breast and thighs, skinned and boneless

2 large red onions, cut in 6 pieces each

18 small red or white potatoes

fresh rosemary

salt and pepper, to taste

½ cup Calamata olives, minced

Sauce for chicken:

3 tablespoons honey

3 tablespoons olive oil

1 cup white wine

Pre-heat oven to 350°. In large flat, oiled dish, put chicken, potatoes, and onions. Using Kosher salt and freshly ground pepper, season chicken and cover with lots of freshly chopped rosemary. Mix together sauce and pour over chicken (heat in microwave, and use solid honey). Cover tightly with lid or foil. Bake for 1 hour. Uncover and add calamata olives, return to oven for 20-30 minutes, or until potatoes are done. Serve with salad or your favorite green vegetable; also serve with hot crusty bread to soak up the juices! This is a great recipe for a very busy hostess. You can make a day before and re-heat.

Shared by Carol Bryce-Buchanan

TINA'S CHICKEN

4 boneless chicken breasts

1 can cream of asparagus soup

1 cup cheddar cheese, shredded

½ cup mayonnaise

Line chicken in a casserole dish. Mix soup, cheese and mayonnaise together. Pour soup mixture over chicken breasts. Bake covered, for 1 hour on 350°. Remove cover, sprinkle a little extra cheese on top and let cook uncovered, for another 10-15 minutes.

Shared by Tina Garrity

JAPANESE RIBS

6 pounds of beef short ribs

Barbecue sauce for marinade

vegetable oil for grilling

Pour sauce over ribs and refrigerate for at least 2 hours, overnight is better. Oil grates and grill ribs over high heat about 10-12 minutes, leave pink on inside.

For the BBQ Sauce:

Whisk all ingredients together, pour over ribs and refrigerate. Marinade can be made up to 2 days in advance.

Shared by Loretta Tallevast

Japanese BBQ Sauce:

1 cup Japanese soy sauce

5 large garlic cloves, chopped

3 tablespoons finely grated fresh ginger

4 scallions, sliced thin, white and green

¼ cup brown sugar

2 tablespoons dark sesame oil

freshly ground black pepper

BEEF BURGUNDY

Put roast in large crock pot on medium heat. Add soup mix, cream of mushroom soup, water and wine. Cover and let cook overnight. In the morning, pull meat apart in pot. Turn pot to low heat and simmer. Two hours before serving, turn to high and stir thoroughly. Pull meat apart again. Prepare egg noodles according to package directions. While noodles are cooking, add sour cream to pot and stir. Serve over noodles.

Shared by Tom Banish

1 package Lipton onion soup mix

1 can condensed cream of mushroom soup

8 ounces water

8 ounces dry red wine

2 pounds top round roast

1 can sliced mushrooms, drained

1 cup sour cream

1 package extra wide egg noodles

HEARTY HAMBURGER CASSEROLE

1½ pounds ground beef
½   cup green pepper, chopped
1⅓ cup onion, chopped
1   tablespoon salt
¼   teaspoon pepper
3   tablespoons butter
1   32 ounce jar spaghetti sauce or homemade sauce
½   cup sour cream
1   cup cottage cheese
1   pound spaghetti
½   pound cream cheese
1   tablespoon poppy seeds

Brown ground beef, onions and peppers with seasonings. Cook spaghetti. Melt cream cheese over low heat and mix with sour cream, cottage cheese and poppy seed. Mix spaghetti with cheese mixture and add to the beef mixture. Grease 3-quart casserole, layer with spaghetti-cheese mixture and beef mixture and spaghetti sauce. Repeat. Bake 350° for 30-35 minutes covered, then continue uncovered for another 15 minutes, until lightly browned. Remove from oven and toss before serving.

Shared by Diane Dolan

MISHE ME PRESHE

1   pound boneless lamb pieces
1   medium onion, chopped
½   green pepper, chopped
3   tomatoes, chopped
1   glove garlic, chopped
1   cup tomato sauce
1   cup water
2   stalks of celery, chopped
1   bunch of leeks, well cleaned and cut into chunks
salt and pepper, to taste
oregano to taste

Sauté lamb pieces in deep pot until lightly browned. Add chopped onion and simmer. Add green pepper, tomatoes and continue to simmer. Add garlic, tomato sauce, water and celery. Continue simmering mixture for ½ hour. Add leeks and seasonings and simmer for another ½ hour. Variation - you can add cauliflower at this point. Best if made a few hours before serving so that all the juices have had a chance to blend.

Shared by Susan Gardner

Gazebo at East Wharf Beach

SCRUMPTIOUS SEAFOOD

Salmon Filet with Strawberry Salsa

Scallop Scampi

Seafood Paella

Noodles' Paella Catalana

Grilled Salmon over Wasabi Mashed Potatoes

Shrimp Scampi

Chilian Sea Bass with Mango Salsa

Swordfish Florentine

Noodles' Crab Cakes

Tilapia in White Wine Sauce

Grilled White Clam Pizza

Ginger Grilled Shrimp

Jambalaya

The Wharf's Tuna Burger

Mussels with White Clam Sauce

Scallops with Veggies, Ginger and Cream Sauce

SCRUMPTIOUS SEAFOOD

SALMON FILET WITH STRAWBERRY SALSA

1 large salmon filet

2 lemons

sprigs of dill, sage or
    other fresh herbs for
    garnish

1 pint strawberries,
    washed thoroughly
    and dried, cut into
    ¼ inch diced pieces

¼ cup balsamic vinegar

1 small jalapeno pepper,
    finely chopped,
    remove insides

¼ teaspoon salt

20 turns freshly ground
    white pepper

1 teaspoon honey

olive oil spray

Preheat oven to 400°. Wash and dry salmon. Without cutting through the skin, slice horizontally into 1½-inch portions. Spray filet with olive oil on both sides and generously salt and pepper. Place in shallow baking pan, and bake for 20-30 minutes, remove from oven.

Meanwhile, put cut up strawberries and jalapenos into a small mixing bowl. Add honey, salt and white pepper. Mix and then add balsamic vinegar and stir until well blended. Cut lemons into wedges. Gently remove salmon from baking pan, leaving the skin in pan. Arrange salmon on platter to resemble a whole fish. Place lemon wedges and herb sprigs around the outside of the salmon. Spoon salsa in a thick strip down the center of the salmon. Serve immediately. This is delicious with steamed spinach and baked sweet potato fries.

Shared by Holly Algood

Salmon Filet with Strawberry Salsa

SCALLOP SCAMPI

½   cup fresh parsley, chopped
¾   stick butter
¼   cup lemon juice
2   tablespoons heavy cream
1   teaspoon salt
1   teaspoon Worcestershire sauce
4   cloves garlic, minced
2   pounds sea scallops
3   teaspoons olive oil
2   plum tomatoes, seeded and chopped
½   cup fresh basil, chopped
¼   dry white wine

Mix first 7 ingredients together in a small bowl to make a broth. In a non-stick skillet, heat 3 teaspoons oil over medium heat. Add scallops and cook for 1-2 minutes per side, turning once. Transfer scallops to the small broth bowl. Add tomatoes, basil and wine to skillet, cook over medium heat for 5 minutes. Stir in butter until melted, remove from heat and add cooked scallops and broth. Serve promptly with rice.

SEAFOOD PAELLA

2   squid, chopped
12   shrimp, peeled and deveined
1   lobster, chopped
small frozen bag of peas
1   red pepper, chopped
3   cups white rice
salt and pepper, to taste
saffron
4   tablespoons olive oil

In a large fry pan, heat the olive oil, add more if needed, and sauté the squid, shrimp and lobster for about 3-4 minutes. In another pot, cook rice in 2 cups water to 1 cup rice. Add cooked rice to seafood mixture. Add saffron and salt and pepper, to taste. To spice this up, sauté garlic and/or onions with seafood. Also, add 2 teaspoons of crushed red pepper to final mixture.

Shared by Sindia Casado Casado

This recipe was given to my family from an exchange student, Sindia, that lived with us for a month this summer, 2005. Her mother makes this for her all the time. She gave it to me in Spanish and then she translated it!!! This is from the region of Navarra. Enjoy!!

NOODLES' PAELLA CATALANA

Steam open clams and mussels, and discard any that won't open. Sauté sausage and chicken in oil with garlic and shallots. Add shrimp and salmon, when shrimp starts to turn pink, add clam juice and wine. Stir in pepper flakes, saffron, oregano, peas and red pepper. Add rice, clams and mussels to broth and cook all of this together for 5 minutes. Divide into two bowls. Spoon over rice and sprinkle top with fresh parsley, this will serve 2.

Shared by Noodles Restaurant

4	large shrimp, peeled and deveined
6	ounces salmon filet, 4 pieces
6	ounces chorizo sausage, ¼ inch discs
6	ounces chicken, ½ inch strips
6	mussels
6	little neck clams
1	cup clam juice
1	cup white wine
½	cup olive oil
2	cloves garlic, minced
2	shallots, minced
1	tablespoon parsley, chopped
1	teaspoon oregano
1	teaspoon saffron threads
	dash hot pepper flakes
½	cup peas
2	ounces red pepper, diced
	Uncle Ben's rice, flavored with saffron, prepared

GRILLED SALMON OVER WASABI MASHED POTATOES

1   stick of butter, unsalted
⅓   cup honey
⅓   cup packed brown sugar
2   tablespoons fresh lemon juice
1   teaspoon natural liquid smoke flavoring
¾   teaspoon crushed dried red pepper flakes
2   pounds center cut salmon filet, skin on

Combine the first 6 ingredients in saucepan, and cook over medium heat, stirring until smooth. Cool. Place salmon in a dish and pour cooled marinade over it. Marinate for 30 minutes, turning salmon once. Heat grill and oil grill grates. Cook the salmon, skin side up for 5-7 minutes and then turn over. Cook for another 5 minutes until fish flakes easily. Remove from grill. Cut salmon into individual portion sizes and serve on top of wasabi mashed potatoes. *Wasabi mashed potatoes recipe on page 64 .

Shared be Kris Moss

SHRIMP SCAMPI

¾   pound medium shrimp, cleaned and deveined
6   tablespoons butter
1   tablespoon scallions
2   tablespoons olive oil
5   garlic cloves, chopped
2   teaspoons lemon juice
¼   teaspoon salt
2   tablespoons parsley, chopped
¼   teaspoon lemon peel

In frying pan mix butter, scallions, olive oil, garlic, lemon juice and salt. Stir until bubbly. Add shrimp. Cook for about 5 minutes or until shrimp are pink on all sides. Add parsley and lemon peel. Serve over rice pilaf or pasta.

The kids always pick this recipe for their special birthday dinner!!

Shared by Janice Florentine

CHILEAN SEA BASS WITH MANGO SALSA

1¾ pound sea bass
olive oil
fresh basil
2 plum tomatoes
1 mango
1 tablespoon brown
   sugar
1 garlic clove
1 tablespoon balsamic
   vinegar
salt and pepper, to taste

Drizzle sea bass with olive oil, salt and pepper, bake at 375° for 20 minutes. Chop plum tomatoes and mango, mix in small bowl, add brown sugar, and small handful of fresh basil. Sauté mixture with a little olive oil and chopped garlic, remove from heat, add balsamic vinegar and top mixture on baked chilean sea bass.

Shared by Liz Wallack

SWORDFISH FLORENTINE

2 ¼ inch thick pieces
   of swordfish
white flour
2 eggs, beaten
olive oil
2 tablespoons butter
1 cup fish stock
1 shot white wine
¼ lemon, squeezed
3 cups fresh spinach
2 tablespoons butter for
   spinach

Press fish into flour and dip into egg mixture. Sauté swordfish in sauce pan, with enough olive oil to coat pan, for about 2 minutes on each side. Move to side. Using another sauce pan, melt 2 tablespoon butter, add fish stock, 1 shot glass of white wine, lemon, salt and pepper, to taste and simmer for 5 minutes with the swordfish. Sauce should thicken up. Meanwhile, wash and remove stems from spinach. Melt butter in another sauce pan and add spinach until wilted, season to taste. Put spinach on platter and cover with swordfish and sauce.

Shared by Joe Coniglialo of Bradley and Wall

NOODLES CRAB CAKES

1 egg
1 cup roasted red pepper puree
1 cup mayonnaise
1 tablespoon Dijon mustard
1 teaspoon Worcestershire sauce
1 teaspoon lemon juice
1 small onion, diced
1 large celery stalk, diced
1 ounce olive oil
1 teaspoon Old Bay seasoning
1 pound leg and claw crabmeat
5 cups Ritz cracker crumbs

Sauté onion and celery in olive oil, sprinkle with Old Bay seasoning. Drain excess oil with strainer. Combine mayo, Dijon mustard, egg, red pepper puree, Worcestershire sauce and lemon juice and add to olive oil mixture. Add crabmeat (careful not to break it apart) and work in the Ritz crackers. Divide into patties and dust with flour. Pan fry until golden brown. Serve immediately.

Shared by Noodles Restaurant

TILAPIA IN WHITE WINE SAUCE

2 pieces of tilapia
¾ cup plain bread crumbs
¼ cup olive oil
2 tablespoons butter
3 scallions, chopped
2 garlic cloves, chopped
2 ounces white wine
⅛ cup chicken stock
⅛ cup fish stock
4 basil leaves, torn
¾ cup marinara sauce
salt and pepper, to taste

Wash fish, (leave wet) press into bread crumbs and sauté in very hot olive oil, about 2 minutes per side. Use enough olive oil to coat the bottom of skillet. Remove fish. Melt butter, add scallions, garlic and fish. Sauté for 2 minutes. Add white wine, chicken stock, fish stock, basil, and salt and pepper. Simmer for 3-4 minutes and then scoop marinara sauce over the fish. Let heat through and serve immediately.

Shared by Joe Coniglialo of Bradley and Wall

GRILLED WHITE CLAM PIZZA

2   Boboli thin crust pizza crusts

¼   cup olive oil

4   tablespoons butter

1   medium onion, chopped

¼   teaspoon black pepper

8   cloves garlic, chopped

½   cup fresh parsley, chopped

20   medium little neck clams (shuck clams raw, reserve juice)

In a large skillet or fry pan, add olive oil, butter and chopped garlic. Sauté until onion is translucent. Add parsley, stir 2-4 minutes, add whole clams and ¼ cup of reserved juice and sauté for about 5-8 minutes (or until clams are cooked.) Set pan aside, and add pepper.

Heat grill at medium setting. Line top of grill with tin foil, brush top of one crust with olive oil and place on tin foil. Heat crust until brown, brush bottom of crust and repeat process on the bottom. Add a few spoonfuls of clam mixture to crust, spreading evenly over the crust. Heat until bubbling. Put onto pizza plate, cool 2-3 minutes, cut with pizza cutter and enjoy!

Shared by Lori Kinne

My husband and I have always taken our family on summer vacations on our bo to Block Island. We all enj clamming together. We all l clams and have eaten them any way we could think of. I came up with this recipe a fe years ago and it was an instant success! I also use th small Boboli crusts at picni and parties and serve the piz as an appetizer. It is a very simple recipe, but always ge great reviews!

Grilled White Clam Pizza

GINGER GRILLED SHRIMP

2 cups soy sauce

4 tablespoons ginger, freshly grated

½ teaspoon salt

½ teaspoon pepper

3 tablespoons extra virgin olive oil, plus more for the grill

2 green onions, finely chopped

2 pounds large shrimp, shelled and deveined

bamboo skewers

Soak skewers in water for 30 minutes. Combine first 6 ingredients and pour over shrimp. Marinate in refrigerator for 30 minutes. Prepare grill to medium heat. Brush grill rack with olive oil. Remove shrimp from marinade and reserve. Skewer shrimp and grill on each side 2-3 minutes until pink, brushing occasionally with reserved marinade. Serve over rice or pasta.

Shared by Laura J. Tichy

I have lived by the shoreline my entire life. I would never be able to live anywhere else, for I enjoy the freedom and peace the ocean brings to me when I look at it. This recipe reminds me of those feelings and how truly lucky I am to continue to live by the sea.

JAMBALAYA

Cook rice using chicken broth instead of water, as per instructions on box. Sauté garlic, shallot in olive oil for 5 minutes on medium heat in a large pot. Add fresh chopped tomatoes, chicken and sausage. Cook 5-10 minutes until almost completely cooked, then add mussels, clams and scallops. Squeeze juice from lemon, and add all herbs and stir. Cook on a very low simmer until the mussels and clams open. Discard any that do not open. Put cooked rice in the bottom of a large baking dish and pour the seafood mixture over the rice. Season with salt and pepper and bake at 350° for 20-30 minutes.

Shared by Liz Wallack

2	boxes Zatarains (jambalaya mix) rice
¼	cup olive oil
4	cloves garlic, chopped
2	shallots, chopped
7	plum tomatoes, chopped
½	cup white wine
1	fresh lemon
4	tablespoons fresh parsley, chopped
4	tablespoons fresh rosemary, chopped
4	tablespoons fresh basil, chopped
2	pounds mussels
2	pounds little neck clams
1	pound large scallops
1	pound large shrimp, peeled and deveined
1	package chorizo or spicy smoked andouille sausage
1	pound chicken, cubed

THE WHARF'S TUNA BURGER

2	pounds fresh tuna (free of skin, gristle and dark flesh)
⅛	cup garlic, minced
¼	cup Dijon mustard
¾	teaspoon cayenne pepper
⅓	teaspoon salt
⅓	teaspoon black pepper

Grind tuna and transfer to stainless steel bowl. Combine tuna with the remaining ingredients and mix thoroughly. Divide into 4 patties and grill until cooked through. Serve with The Wharf's ginger mustard glaze.

Glaze:
Combine all ingredients and bring to a boil in sauce pan. Reduce and lower to simmer for 5 minutes.

Shared by The Wharf

Ginger mustard Glaze

½	cup teriyaki sauce
¼	cup fresh ginger, minced
¾	teaspoon garlic, mince
⅛	cup honey
⅛	cup Dijon mustard
1	teaspoon white wine vinegar

MUSSELS WITH WHITE CLAM SAUCE

¼	stick butter
4	tablespoons olive oil
¼	cup white wine
1	small can clam juice
handful	fresh chopped parsley
10	sundried tomatoes, chopped
handful	fresh cilantro
sprinkle	of crushed red pepper
1	fresh lemon
¼	cup parmesan cheese
4	pounds fresh mussels
3	garlic cloves, chopped
1	small shallot, chopped

In a large pot, add butter, olive oil, garlic and shallot. Then add mussels, clam juice, white wine, ¼-teaspoon crushed red pepper. Squeeze fresh lemon juice from lemon into mixture and cook for 10 minutes. Add chopped sundried tomatoes and add olive oil, cilantro and fresh parsley. Cook over low heat until mussels open. Sprinkle parmesan cheese over top and serve with Italian bread.

Shared by Liz Wallack

The Wharf's Tuna Burger

SCALLOPS WITH VEGETABLES, GINGER AND CREAM SAUCE

4 tablespoons butter

1 small turnip, cut into matchstick-sized strips

1 large red pepper, cut into matchstick-sized strips

1 large carrot, cut into matchstick-sized strips

1 tablespoon peeled fresh ginger, minced

1 large zucchini, cut into matchstick-sized strips

20 large sea scallops

¾ cups whipping cream

Melt 2 tablespoons butter in a heavy large skillet over medium heat. Add turnip, red pepper, carrot and ginger and cover and cook for 3 minutes. Add zucchini and sauté uncovered for another 3 minutes until the veggies are crisp and tender. Season to taste with salt and pepper and set aside. Melt 1 tablespoon butter in a different heavy large skillet over medium-high heat. Working in small batches, sauté scallops until cooked through, add more butter as needed. Transfer scallops to plate and cover with tin foil. Add cream to skillet, increase heat to boil the cream (boil for about 3 minutes). Season with salt and pepper. Divide veggies among 4 plates, mounding veggies in the center of each plate. Place 5 scallops in a circular fashion around the veggies and spoon cream sauce over scallops.

Shared by Jen Walker

Jake's corn stand

BREAKFAST, BRUNCH AND BREAD

Papa's Corn Pancakes

Karen's Banana Chip Bread

Prize Biscuits

Caren's Biscotti

Cinnamon Rolls

Mrs. Keener's Pumpkin Bread

To Die For Blueberry Muffins

Raspberry Sauce

Grand Mariner Orange French Toast

Sunday Morning Raisin Bread

Orange Syrup

Buttery Corn Bread

Irish Bread

Cinnamon French Toast Souffle

Fresh Tomato Basil Quiche

Tidewater Pie Pastry Dough

Terri's Never Fail Lobster Quiche

Delicious Dill Bread

BREAKFAST, BRUNCH AND BREAD

PAPA'S CORN PANCAKES

2 cups Aunt Jemima's
  pancake mix
2 cups milk
2 eggs, beaten
1 8 ounce can, whole
  kernel corn, drained
  of liquid

Mix all ingredients together. Spray skillet with cooking spray. Drop batter by ladle full on skillet that is on medium high heat. When batter starts to bubble slightly, flip pancakes. Top cooked side with pad of butter. Serve promptly with maple syrup or molasses. Makes 10-12 pancakes.

Shared by John Carroll

I have been making these pancakes for my children and their friends for over 40 years!

KAREN'S BANANA CHIP BREAD

3 eggs, well beaten
½ cup applesauce
¾ cup canola oil
1 cup sugar
1 heaping tablespoon
  pure vanilla extract
¼ cup light brown sugar
1½ cups all-purpose flour
½ teaspoon cinnamon
1 teaspoon baking soda
3 rotten bananas
½ cup semi-sweet
  chocolate chips
dash of salt

Heat oven to 350°. Grease 11 x 7-inch pan. Mix eggs, applesauce, oil, sugars, and vanilla in a bowl. In a separate bowl, mix flour, salt, cinnamon and baking soda. Add the dry ingredients to the egg mixture and mix well. Add bananas and continue mixing. Pour into pan, and sprinkle chocolate chips over the top. Bake 30 minutes or until toothpick comes clean. Cool before cutting into bite size pieces.

Shared by Karen L. Anderson

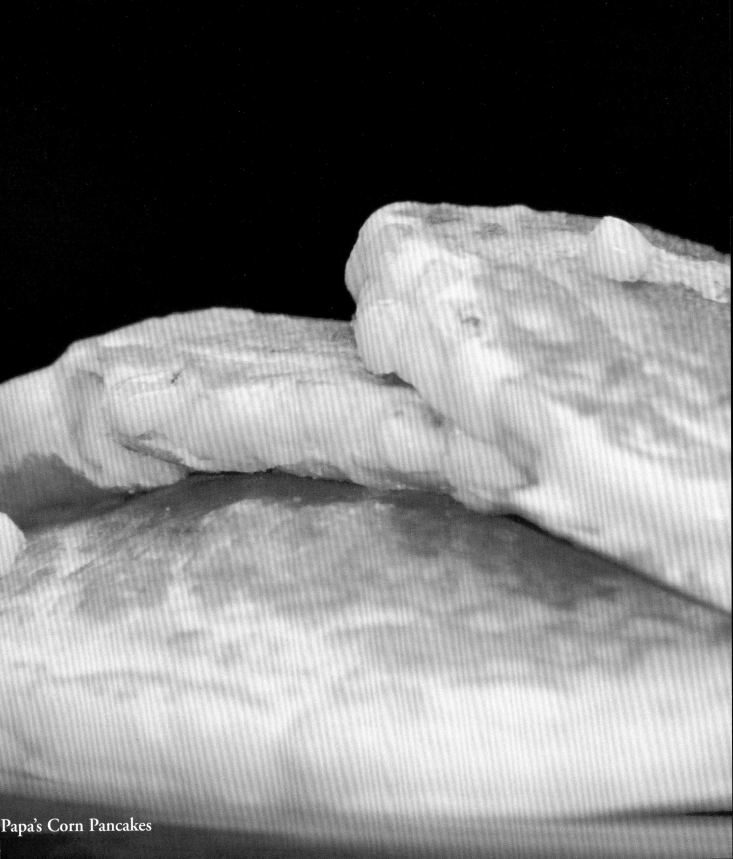

Papa's Corn Pancakes

PRIZE BISCUITS

2 cups flour
2 teaspoons sugar
½ teaspoon cream of tartar
½ cup shortening plus 1 tablespoon
4 teaspoons baking powder
½ teaspoon salt
¾ cup milk

Mix all ingredients together, and form into medium-size balls. Bake for 10-12 minutes at 450°.

Shared by Annie Auerbach

My Dad's mother died when was 20. Although I never me her, I always heard about Grandma Karla's famous biscuits. Every summer my mother would bake a batch a she would let us have strawb shortcake with homemade whipped cream for dinner.

CAREN'S BISCOTTI

2 cups flour
1 cup sugar
1 teaspoon baking powder
1 teaspoon vanilla
dash of salt
3 eggs
1 cup almonds, chopped
½ cup pistachios, chopped (shelled), can substitute with almonds

Beat the eggs and vanilla. Add nuts to dry ingredients, then turn dry ingredients into the egg mixture. Rest the dough while you pre-heat oven at 300°. Spray a cookie shee with Pam, then make 3 loaves on the cookie sheet (use floured hands to make loaves) Bake 30-40 minutes. While hot, slice at an angle. Put slices back on their sides and continue cooking for 20-25 minutes. Whatever you want to add as extras are welcome you can use walnuts, or mini chocolate morsels. Try dried fruit, such as cherries or raisins! Be sure to mix the extras in the dough before cooking. These freeze wonderfully The only thing missing is a glass of milk or cup of tea!

Shared by Caren Smith Israel

Prize Biscuits

CINNAMON ROLLS

2 cups lukewarm water
½ cup sugar
1½ teaspoons salt
2 yeast cakes
1 egg
¼ cup shortening or soft
   margarine
7 cups flour
1 stick butter, melted
cinnamon-sugar mixture
½ cup sugar
½ cup cinnamon

Mix water, sugar, and salt until dissolved. Crumble yeast into this mixture, stir and let dissolve 5 minutes. Stir in egg, shortening, and then ½ of the flour. Mix well and add the rest of the flour, ½ cup at a time, until dough is only slightly sticky. Let rise in refrigerator and punch down. Shape into cinnamon rolls by taking a golf-ball sized piece of dough, roll between palms until 5 inches long. Dip in melted butter, then cinnamon sugar mixture and place in baking pan. Cover and refrigerate overnight, remove in a.m. Let rise and bake at 350° for 25 minutes.

Shared by Jeanette Hogue

Our family enjoys these cinnamon rolls every Christm... morning, and it all started 22 years ago. That was the first time I ever tasted them. Jim and I were dating, when he m... a huge pan of them to share w... my family that Christmas. They were still warm when he brought them to our house! M... mother was impressed to say t... least, but it was my three siste... who pulled me aside and said, "Okay Jeanette, hang onto th... guy, he's a keeper." And, that'... just what I did!

*Mrs. Beverly Keener was a teacher at Island Avenue Elementary School
for many years and this is the pumpkin bread recipe she used for the classroom to enjoy.
Not only is it delicious, but it brings back fond memories of a wonderful educator!
A long time resident of Madison, her children graduated
from Daniel Hand High School. She now resides in
North Branford and is busy being a grandma.*

MRS. KEENER'S PUMPKIN BREAD

Beat eggs until foamy. Add sugar, oil and vanilla. Beat until thick. Stir in pumpkin, all dry ingredients and raisins and pour into 2 greased loaf pans. Bake at 350° for 50-60 minutes.

Shared by Susan Ciotti Wivell

3	eggs
2	cups sugar
1	cup vegetable oil
1	teaspoon vanilla
2	cups flour
1	teaspoon cinnamon
1	teaspoon baking soda
1	teaspoon salt
½	teaspoon baking powder
1	cup raisins
2	cups pumpkin, cooked or canned

TO DIE FOR BLUEBERRY MUFFINS

1½ cups all-purpose flour
½ cup sugar
¼ cup brown sugar
½ teaspoon salt
2 teaspoons baking powder
⅓ cup vegetable oil
1 egg
⅓ cup milk
1 teaspoon REAL vanilla
1 cup fresh blueberries

Crumb topping:
½ cup sugar
⅓ cup all-purpose flour
¼ cup butter, cubed
1½ teaspoons ground cinnamon

Pre-heat oven to 400°. Grease muffin cups or line with muffin liners. Combine 1½ cups flour, both sugars, salt and baking powder. In a separate bowl mix egg, milk and vanilla. Add this to flour mixture. Fold in blueberries. Fill muffins cups right to the top, and sprinkle with crumb topping.

Crumb topping:
Mix together ½ cup sugar, ⅓ cup flour, ¼ cup butter and 1½ teaspoons cinnamon. Mix with fork, and sprinkle over muffins before baking. Bake for 20-25 minutes in preheated oven, or until done. Makes 8 large muffins.

Shared by Terri Hotchkiss from The Wharf

To Die for Blueberry Muffins

RASPBERRY SAUCE

½ cup sugar

1½ teaspoons cornstarch

2 tablespoons orange juice

12 ounce bag of frozen raspberries, thawed

½ cup fresh whole raspberries

In a heavy saucepan, stir together, sugar and cornstarch. Add orange juice, stir until smooth. Add previously frozen raspberries and cook over medium heat. Stir constantly until mixture thickens and boils. Serve with fresh raspberries as a garnish.

Shared by Victoria Kolyvas, Innkeeper, Tidewater Inn

GRAND MARNIER ORANGE FRENCH TOAST

4 large eggs

¾ cup half and half

¼ cup Grand Marnier

2 tablespoons sugar

1 tablespoon fresh grated orange peel or 1 teaspoon dried

½ teaspoon vanilla extract

1 large loaf Challah bread

powdered sugar

maple syrup

Whisk together eggs, half and half, Grand Marnier, sugar, orange peel and vanilla extract. Slice Challah bread crosswise, on the diagonal into ¾ inch slices. Dip each bread slice into the egg mixture and arrange slices in a 10 x 15 inch glass baking dish. Pour remaining egg mixture over the bread slices and cover with plastic wrap and refrigerate overnight, allowing bread to absorb egg mixture completely. Cook bread on buttered grill or skillet on medium heat for 3 minutes per side. Put on plates and sprinkle with powdered sugar and serve with maple syrup. This will serve 4-6 people. Also serve with raspberry sauce or orange syrup.

Shared by Victoria Kolyvas, Innkeeper, Tidewater Inn

Tidewater Inn's Raspberry Sauce and Orange Syrup

SUNDAY MORNING RAISIN BREAD

3	tablespoons butter
1	cup sugar
¾	cup raisins
1	tablespoon lemon rind, grated
3	cups flour
3	eggs
3	teaspoons baking powder
1	teaspoon salt
¼	teaspoon mace
½	teaspoon lemon extract
1	cup milk
½	teaspoon vanilla

Grease and flour 9 x 5 x 3 loaf pan. Preheat oven to 350°. Cream butter and sugar; add one egg at a time beating well after each addition. Stir in raisins and lemon rind. Mix and sift together dry ingredients. Combine lemon extract, vanilla and milk together. Mix dry ingredients with milk mixture. Add to raisin mixture. Pour into loaf pan and bake at 350° for approximately 45-50 minutes.

Enjoy with butter or jam and a hot cup of coffee!

Shared by Audrey Weber

ORANGE SYRUP

¾	cup frozen orange juice concentrate
½	cup sweet butter
½	cup sugar
	freshly grated nutmeg, to taste
	mandarin orange segments, to garnish

In a heavy saucepan, warm together orange juice, sweet butter and sugar. Be careful not to boil. Add nutmeg to taste and garnish with a few mandarin orange segments.

Shared by Victoria Kolyvas, Innkeeper, Tidewater Inn

Sunday Morning Raisin Bread

BUTTERY CORN BREAD

⅔ cup butter
1 cup sugar
3 eggs
1⅔ cups milk
2⅓ cups flour
1 cup corn meal
4½ teaspoons baking powder
1 teaspoon salt

Cream butter and sugar. In a separate bowl combine eggs and milk. In another bowl combine flour, cornmeal, baking powder and salt. Add flour mixture to butter mixture, alternately with egg mixture. Bake in greased 13 x 9 x 2 pan. Bake at 400° for 22-27 minutes.

Shared by Marla Lewis

IRISH BREAD

3 eggs
½ cup sugar
3 cups flour
½ teaspoon salt
1¾ teaspoon baking powder
1 cup milk
2 tablespoons oil
3 teaspoons caraway seeds
1 cup raisins

Grease 9-inch loaf pan. Beat eggs and sugar, add flour, salt, and baking powder. Mix while slowly adding milk and oil. Fold in caraway seeds and raisins. Bake at 350° for 1 hour.

Shared by Terri Messier

My maternal grandfather gr[e]w up in Ireland and brought th[e] recipe over to America when h[e] came to Ellis Island as a you[ng] man. My grandmother woul[d] make this delicious bread on my family visits when I was growing up. My mother continued making the Irish bread, especially on St. Patrick's Day and Easter. I now make this bread with my three daughters!

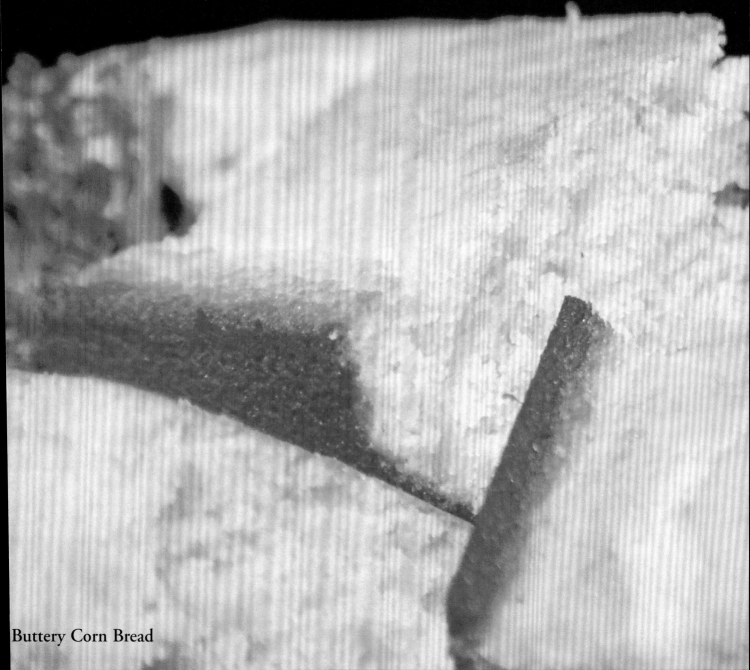

Buttery Corn Bread

CINNAMON FRENCH TOAST SOUFFLE

1 **large loaf cinnamon bread, cubed to fit a 13x9 pan**

12 **ounces cream cheese, softened**

6 **ounces butter, softened**

¾ **cup maple syrup, divided ¼ cup and ½ cup**

10 **eggs**

3 **cups half and half**

cinnamon sugar

buttered maple syrup (50/50 mix of butter and ½ of the maple syrup)

powdered sugar

Place bread in well-buttered pan. Mix cream cheese, butter, plus ¼ cup maple syrup until smooth. Spread on top of bread, leaving holes through which to pour egg mixture. Beat eggs, half and half and ½ cup maple syrup. Pour over bread and sprinkle with cinnamon sugar. Cover and refrigerate overnight. Uncover and bake 50-55 for minutes at 350°. Cut into squares and sprinkle with powdered sugar. Serves 8.

Shared by Sue Zaccagnino

One of our Christmas traditions is to prepare a Christmas morning breakfast casserole the day before and have it cooking while the family opens gifts. This one is especially delicious!

Cinnamon French Toast Souffle

The Tidewater Inn has hosted guests of Madison families for over 20 years.
The Fresh Tomato-Basil Quiche recipe combines the freshest flavors of summer.
Because of the rave reviews from our guests, this dish is frequently
offered on summer weekends.

FRESH TOMATO BASIL QUICHE

4   large eggs, beaten

2   cups heavy cream

½   teaspoon Greek oregano

¼   teaspoon salt

¼   teaspoon pepper

2   medium ripe tomatoes, diced

1   medium ripe tomato, sliced for garnish

1   8 ounce ball of fresh mozzarella cheese, diced

8   basil leaves, shredded

2   tablespoons parmesan cheese, grated

1   cup Monterey Jack cheese, shredded

paprika

Tidewater Pie Pastry Dough

⅓   cup lard

1   cup unsifted unbleached flour, such as King Arthur

⅓   cup cold milk

To make the dough, cut the lard into the flour with a pastry blender or two dinner knives until the mixture resembles coarse bread crumbs. Add milk slowly and mix with a fork until the dough is soft and forms a ball. Wrap dough ball in plastic wrap and chill in refrigerator for at least 30 minutes. This can be made up to 2 days ahead. Makes one pie crust. Roll out and line the pie dish. Crimp or flute the top edge all around. Put in refrigerator to chill completely as you prepare the filling.

Toss together diced tomatoes, mozzarella cheese and shredded basil. Put all ingredients in the bottom of prepared pie shell. Spread the shredded monterey jack evenly overall. Pour egg mixture over. Arrange the tomato slices on top, interspaced with whole basil leaves. Sprinkle with grated parmesan cheese and paprika.

Bake at 425° for 15 minutes. Reduce oven temperature to 350° and continue baking for 45-60 minutes, until golden on top and nearly completely set in the center. Remove from oven and let sit at least 15 minutes before cutting and serving.

Shared by Victoria Kolyvas, Innkeeper, The Tidewater Inn

Tidewater Pie Pastry Dough

TERRI'S NEVER FAIL LOBSTER QUICHE

¼ **pound fresh lobster meat**
5 **eggs**
1 **pint heavy cream**
¼ **cup parmesan cheese**
¼ **cup sour cream**
salt and pepper, to taste

In a large bowl, mix all ingredients together. Choose your favorite ingredients to add to lobster including, ham, bacon, onion, spinach, or tomato. Add your favorite cheese, like Swiss, dill havarti, cheddar or monterey. Preheat oven to 325°. On a baking sheet, crimp edges of crust and brush with egg wash and bake for 18 minutes. Fill pie crusts ¾ way up with lobster mixture and top with your choice of additional fillings. Bake for approximately 45 minutes until brown and set. Serve with side salad and fruit.

Shared by Terri Hotchkiss of The Wharf

DELICIOUS DILL BREAD

1 **package dry yeast**
¼ **cup water**
1 **cup cottage cheese (small curd, creamed and heated to luke warm)**
2 **tablespoons sugar**
1 **tablespoon dried onion**
2 **tablespoons dill seed**
¼ **teaspoon baking soda**
1 **egg, unbeaten**
2¼ **cups flour**
1 **tablespoon butter**
1 **teaspoon salt**

Soften yeast in ¼ cup water warmed to 120° in which sugar has been dissolved. Allow to grow for 30 minutes. Combine yeast with all ingredients except butter, salt and flour. Add butter and salt, then add flour. Bread will be very sticky. Wipe a bowl with vegetable oil, place bread dough in bowl, turning until bread dough is covered thinly with oil. Turn into 8-inch greased round casserole dish. Let rise for 40 minutes. Bake for 40-50 minutes at 350°. When cooked through, brush top with melted butter and sprinkle with salt. Serve with whipped butter.

Shared by Audrey Weber

Terri's Never Fail Lobster Quiche

SWEET THINGS

Gram's Chocolate Chip Cookies
Scotch Shortbread
Yummy Chocolate Chip Mandel Bread
Martha's Brittle Cookies
Potato Candy
Key Lime Sugar Cookies
Sugar Cookies
Australian Pavlova
Lace Cookies
Bob's Cheesecake
Amaretto Mousse Trifle
Daffodil Cake
Kentucky Butter Cake
Chris's Cheesecake
Chocolate Chip Bundt Cake
Mud Pie
Congo Bars
Melt In Your Mouth Blueberry Cake
Graham Cracker Brownies
Nancy's Whoopie Pie
Susan's 14 Carrot Cake
Lazy Daisy Cake
Black Bottom Pie

SWEET THINGS

GRAM'S CHOCOLATE CHIP COOKIES

¾ stick Crisco shortening

1¼ cup packed light brown sugar

2 tablespoons milk

1 tablespoon vanilla

1 egg

1¾ cups all-purpose flour

1 teaspoon salt

¾ teaspoon baking soda

1½ cups semi-sweet chocolate chips

Combine Crisco, brown sugar, milk and vanilla in large bowl. Beat in egg. Combine flour, salt, and baking soda, mix into Crisco mixture until blended. Stir in chocolate chips. Drop rounded tablespoons of dough 3-inches apart on an ungreased cookie sheet. Bake at 375° for 8-10 minutes for chewy cookies and 11-12 minutes for crispy cookies.

Shared by June Jean

This recipe is a favorite of all my grandchildren. I have made them for years, same as my mother who was known for her famous cookies. I estimate that I have made 1,000 dozen cookies for hockey teams, soccer teams, bake sales, and every family gathering we have ever had!!! Enjoy!

SCOTCH SHORTBREAD

1 pound butter

1 cup sugar

4 cups sifted flour

Mix ingredients together. Press onto cookie sheet that has an outer edge or sides using hands, pressing the batter to cover cookie sheet. Make sure surface is smooth and covered. Prick entire surface with a fork. Bake for ½ hour at 300°. Turn oven down to 250° and keep cooking shortbread until golden brown. Cut while warm into finger-size bars.

Shared by Karen Greenberg

YUMMY CHOCOLATE CHIP MANDEL BREAD

Every November my Dad is off to his Florida home to spend the winter until early June. He enjoys the warm weather there, but misses his family at home. So I like to send him memories of home while he is away. Mandel bread, a traditional Jewish dessert is the perfect care package for Dad.

Mix all ingredients together. Form 3 loaves on cookie sheet. Bake at 350° for 20 minutes, until lightly golden. When cool, sprinkle with powdered sugar. Slice on the diagonal.

Shared by Lisa McAndrews

1	stick melted butter
¾	cup sugar
2	eggs
1	teaspoon vanilla
2	cups flour
2	teaspoons baking powder
1	cup walnuts, optional
½	cup coconut, shredded
1	cup chocolate chip mini morsels

MARTHA'S BRITTLE COOKIES

1 cup butter
1 cup brown sugar
40 saltine crackers
12 ounces chocolate chips
chopped nuts (optional)

Line a jelly roll pan with foil. Place the saltines down on the foil. Boil the butter and brown sugar for 3 minutes. Pour butter mixture over saltines. Bake at 350° for 5 minutes. Sprinkle chocolate chips over cookies and spread around. Sprinkle with nuts. Cool and peel off foil. Break apart to form brittle cookies.

Shared by Tammy Stemen

These cookies are an eternal family favorite for both kids and adults alike. My grandmother, Martha Mattson, used to make them for us, now my sister, Tracy Johnston and I, carry on the tradition. These cookies were popular when times were "hard" because the list of ingredients is so short.

POTATO CANDY

1 medium potato, cooked
4 tablespoons butter
dash salt
2 teaspoons vanilla extract
2 pounds confectioners sugar
1 bag coconut flakes
1 bag chocolate chips
1 teaspoon Crisco

Mash potato with butter until smooth, salt to taste. Add sugar to the first three ingredients, along with the bag of coconut, mix until firm. Press into a 9x9 buttered pan. Melt the chocolate chips with the Crisco. Pour over pressed candy. Cool and cut into squares.

Shared by Annie Auerbach

This recipe originated during the Great Depression. My grandmother had 21 grandchildren. Every Christmas we all looked forward to each getting our own pan of this candy. Gram would save her aluminum pot pie plates all year to put the candy into.

Martha's Brittle Cookies

KEY LIME SUGAR COOKIES

1   cup butter, chilled
1½ cups sugar
1   egg
1   teaspoon vanilla
2   tablespoons key lime juice
½   teaspoon salt
1½ teaspoons baking powder
2½ cups flour
green and yellow food coloring
green colored sprinkles

Cream butter and sugar until smooth in a mixer, keep mixing and add egg, vanilla and key lime juice. Sift and mix flour and baking powder together. Add to the butter-sugar mixture and mix. Add food coloring to make your favorite color of lime green. Form dough into 2-3 solid logs and wrap in plastic wrap, place in refrigerator or freezer until firm. Cut cookies 1¼-inch thick and place on buttered cookie sheet. Cover with sugar sprinkles. Bake at 350° for 8-10 minutes, until edges are lightly browned. For crunchy cookies bake longer. Dough can be frozen for up to one month before use.

Shared by Carmen Jane Booth

SUGAR COOKIES

1   cup butter
1   cup oil
1   cup sugar
1   cup powered sugar
1   teaspoon vanilla
2   eggs
4   cups flour
1   teaspoon salt
1   teaspoon baking soda
1   teaspoon cream of tartar

Cream together first 4 ingredients. Add remaining ingredients. Roll into balls and flatten with glass dipped in sugar (regular or colored sugar). Bake on ungreased cookie sheet at 375° for 10 minutes.

Shared by Diane Dolan

Key Lime Sugar Cookies

AUSTRALIAN PAVLOVA

6   egg whites
pinch of salt
4   ounces sugar
4   ounces castor sugar
1   teaspoon white vinegar
½   teaspoon vanilla
2   level teaspoons corn flour
fruit, such as strawberries, peaches, blueberries

Preheat oven to 400°. Lightly grease baking tray, then line with baking paper or coat baking tray with cooking spray. Beat egg whites with salt until stiff. Continue beating egg whites and add sugars, vanilla and vinegar until the consistency is thick. Lightly fold in corn flour. Mold mixture into a circular shape (on baking tray), leaving a hollow center in the middle for filling. Turn oven temperature down to 250° and bake pavlova for 1½ hours. Turn oven off and leave pavlova in oven until it cools. Fill center with fruit of your choice and top with whipped cream.

Shared by Jocelyn Cunningham

The "Aussies" claim that in 1935, one of the great chefs created the pavlova to celebrate the visit of the great Russian ballerina, Anna Pavlova. Over the years, the dessert has been adopted as a national recipe...very often enjoyed with the famous summer barbecue. As they say, "Nothing like a wad of juicy meat, washed down with a pint, followed by a Pav.

LACE COOKIES

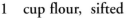

1   cup flour, sifted
1   cup pecans or walnuts, chopped
½   cup light corn syrup
½   cup butter
½   cup firmly packed brown sugar
1   teaspoon vanilla

Mix flour and nuts, set aside. In a heavy saucepan, combine, syrup, butter and sugar. Bring to a boil over medium heat, stirring constantly. Remove from heat and gradually blend in flour and nut mixture. Add vanilla. Drop small spoonfuls of batter on a coated cookie sheet. Bake at 350° for 8-10 minutes.

Shared by Diane Daych.

BOB'S CHEESECAKE

Line bottom and half way up the sides of spring form pan with graham cracker crust. Beat cheese until creamy. Then add sugar, salt, vanilla and flour. Continue to beat until creamy. Add eggs, one at a time and be sure to continue beating after each addition. Add egg yolks and keep beating mixture. Add heavy cream and gently mix. Pour mixture into prepared spring form pan. Bake for 12 minutes on 500° or until golden on top. After 12 minutes, reduce oven temperature to 200° and continue to bake for one hour. Refrigerate for several hours or overnight. Decorate as desired.

This is a very rich cake that we make and savor at Christmas time or any other special holiday.

Shared by Wilma Maus

5   8-ounce packages cream cheese
1¾ cups sugar
¼   teaspoon salt
¼   teaspoon vanilla
3   tablespoons flour
5   eggs
2   egg yolks
¼   cup heavy cream
graham cracker crust, prepare as instructed on package of graham cracker crumbs

AMARETTO MOUSSE TRIFLE

Cube pound cake and sprinkle evenly with Amaretto. In a small bowl, combine milk and pudding mix. Beat this mixture at low speed for 1-2 minutes. Let pudding stand for 5 minutes to thicken. Fold 1½ cups of whipped cream into pudding. Spoon ⅓ of pudding mixture into bottom of 2½-quart straight sided, clear glass, trifle bowl. Add ⅓ of cake cubes on top of pudding. Repeat layers 3 more times, forming 3 layers of alternated pudding and cake. Spread remaining whipped cream over top and sprinkle with chocolate swirls and sliced almonds. Refrigerate until serving time. This can be made one day ahead.

Shared by Susan Miller

1   prepared pound cake
4   tablespoons Amaretto
1½ cups cold whole milk
1   4 ounce package chocolate instant pudding
2   cups whipping cream, whipped
chocolate swirls
sliced almonds

DAFFODIL CAKE

6 egg whites
¾ cup sugar
¼ teaspoon cream of tartar
¼ teaspoon salt
½ cup cake flour
few drops of almond extract
½ teaspoon vanilla extract

6 egg yolks
¾ cup sugar
Pinch of salt
¾ cup cake flour
1 teaspoon baking powder
½ teaspoon vanilla
½ cup boiling water

Frosting:
6 tablespoons butter
1½ tablespoons orange rind, grated
3 cups confectioners sugar
dash of salt
¼ cup orange juice

Beat egg whites with salt and cream of tartar until stiff, but not dry. Fold in sugar and flour (that has been sifted together). Add almond and vanilla extracts. Put mixture in tube pan.

Beat egg yolks, sugar and salt together until lemon colored. Add flour and baking powder, alternately with boiling water. Add vanilla. Pour mixture on top of egg white mixture and swirl gently, but not thoroughly. Bake at 325° for 50 minutes. Turn upside down and cool for 1 hour.

Frosting:
Cream butter and orange rind until soft. Add sugar alternately with orange juice, and salt, beating well after each addition, until smooth. This will cover top and sides of 10-inch tube cake.

Shared by Eleanor Jones

I first enjoyed this cake at my great aunt's house in Maine on my 4th birthday. It became my annual birthday cake, and that of several of my cousins.

Daffodil Cake

KENTUCKY BUTTER CAKE

Cake:

1	cup butter, softened
2	cups sugar
1	cup buttermilk
1	teaspoon baking powder
4	eggs
2	teaspoons vanilla
3	cups flour
½	teaspoon baking soda
1	teaspoon salt

Butter sauce:

1	cup sugar
½	cup water
½	cup butter
1	teaspoon vanilla

Grease bottom only of a 10-inch tube pan. In a large bowl, cream butter at high speed. Gradually add sugar while continuing to cream until mixture is light and fluffy. Add eggs, one at a time, beating after each addition. Add remaining ingredients and blend at low speed until completely mixed. Beat for a final 2 minutes and pour into pan. Bake cake for 60-65 minutes (until top springs back when touched) at 325°. When cake is cooked, remove from oven and prick with fork all over the top. Pour butter sauce over warm cake. Cool completely before removing from pan.

Butter sauce:
Combine all ingredients in pan over low heat. Pour butter sauce over warm cake. Sprinkle cake with confectioners sugar.

Shared by Anne Galinsky

My mother used to bake this cake for us in the summertime. I remember her cooling the cake outside and smelling it while we ran around the neighborhood. When I bake the cake today, the smell brings back wonderful childhood memories.

Kentucky Butter Cake

CHRIS'S CHEESECAKE

4 8 ounce packages
   cream cheese
1 cup sugar
4 eggs
vanilla, to taste
¾ cup melted butter
1 package Oreo cookies,
   crushed

Cream together first 4 ingredients. In a medium cheesecake pan, put in crushed Oreos and pour melted butter on top. With your hands, mix the cookies and butter and form a crust. Pour the creamed mixture over this and bake at 350° for 1 hour. The key is not to over bake a cheesecake. Be careful not to let it set too firmly. After it is cooled, slice fresh fruit and arrange on top of cheesecake.

Shared by Diane Gardner

CHOCOLATE CHIP BUNDT CAKE

1 cup butter
1 cup sour cream
2 cups sugar
2 eggs
½ teaspoon vanilla
2 cups flour
1½ teaspoons baking
   powder
¼ teaspoon salt
1 cup chopped nuts
1 cup chocolate chips

Cream together first 5 ingredients. Sift together flour, baking powder and salt. Add dry ingredients to butter mixture. Mix until creamy. Stir in chopped nuts and chocolate chips. Place mixture in a greased and floured 10-inch tube or bundt pan. Bake for approximately 1 hour on 350°.

Shared by Marla Lewis

This recipe was given to me many years ago by my dear friend, Jackie. The cake has been a success continuously and so, I have shared the recipe with many friends throughout the years. Enjoy!

Chris's Cheesecake

MUD PIE

Pie:

18 Oreo cookies, crushed

½ stick of butter

½ gallon, coffee ice cream, softened

Mix Oreo crumbs and butter together. Press this mixture into the bottom of a greased 10-inch pie shell. Chill. Fill with softened ice cream and freeze.

To make the sauce, add all ingredients to a sauce pan and cook over low heat. Eventually bring to a boiling point. Pour chocolate sauce over frozen pie, top with nuts and whipped cream, if desired.

Shared by Diane Dolan

Chocolate sauce:

¼ cup butter

1 square baking chocolate

¼ cup cocoa

¾ cup sugar

½ cup evaporated milk

dash of salt

1 teaspoon vanilla

CONGO BARS

1½ sticks butter, melted

2¼ cups brown sugar

3 eggs

2⅔ cups flour

2½ teaspoons baking powder

½ teaspoon salt

1 cup walnuts, chopped

1 cup chocolate chips

Stir butter and brown sugar. Add eggs one at a time. Mix flour, baking powder and salt and slowly add to butter mixture. Stir thoroughly. Add walnuts and chocolate chips. Pour into greased 9 x 13-inch greased pan. Bake for 25-30 minutes at 350°. Cut into 2 inch squares.

Shared by Barbara Ciotti

This a favorite with all ages. And the bars pack up great for tailgating parties!

Mud Pie

Just an "old Maine recipe" is how my grandmother described her cooking if I asked her about a particular favorite of mine. One day she bought me a copy of Marjorie Standish's, "Cooking Down East," which is a collection of all the old Maine recipes that I knew from my childhood. Mrs. Standish was well known in Maine because she worked for the electric company and demonstrated in-home cooking when people, including my grandmother, first converted to electric ranges. Later, she wrote for a column for the newspaper where she shared many Maine recipes. The credit for the blueberry cake recipe goes to Mrs.Standish, with much love to my grandmother for her patience while I watched from the stool in her kitchen.

MELT-IN-YOUR-MOUTH-BLUEBERRY CAKE

2 eggs, separated
1 cup sugar
¼ teaspoon salt
½ cup shortening
1 teaspoon vanilla
1½ cups sifted flour
1 teaspoon baking powder
⅓ cup milk
1½ cups fresh blueberries, washed, patted dry and coated very lightly with flour

Beat egg whites until stiff. Add about ¼ cup of the sugar to keep them stiff. In another bowl, cream shortening and add salt and vanilla. Add sifted dry ingredients alternating with the milk (to the shortening mixture). Fold in beaten egg whites and fold in fresh blueberries. Pour mixture into a greased 8 x 8-inch pan. Sprinkle top of batter lightly with remaining sugar. Bake for 50-60 minutes at 350°.

Shared by Laura Downes

GRAHAM CRACKER BROWNIES

My mother cut this recipe out of the "New Haven Register" over 40 years ago! Our family has been enjoying these brownies ever since.

Mix all ingredients except confectioners sugar together, batter will be very stiff. Press batter into a 9-inch square, greased pan. Bake for 25 minutes at 350°. Remove from oven, sprinkle brownies with confectioners sugar while still hot. Cut into squares.

Shared by Betty-Lou Morawski.

1½ cups graham cracker crumbs
1 can condensed milk
1 teaspoon vanilla
1 cup chocolate morsels
1 cup walnuts, chopped
dash of salt
confectioners sugar

NANCY'S WHOOPIE PIE

Pies:
2 cups flour
½ teaspoon salt
1 teaspoon baking soda
⅓ cup cocoa
1 cup sugar
⅓ cup butter, melted
¾ cup milk
1 teaspoon vanilla
1 egg

To make pies, sift together first 4 ingredients, add sugar, butter, milk, vanilla and egg. Mix by hand. Drop spoonfuls on cookie sheet and bake at 350° for 10-12 minutes. Mix together all ingredients for filling and spoon between 2 cooled pies to form whoopie pies.

This is a classic New England favorite. When I was a little girl, my mom used this old, traditional recipe to make whoopie pies. They were great then and still are! Enjoy!!

Shared by Nancy Karas

Filling:
¼ pound softened butter
1 cup confectioners sugar
1 teaspoon vanilla
5 heaping tablespoons fluff

SUSAN'S 14 CARROT CAKE

Blend oil and sugar, beat in eggs one at a time. Sift in dry ingredients. Mix in carrots. Pour into 3 individual 9 inch pans that have been greased and floured. Bake 20-25 minutes at 350° until toothpick comes out clean. Cool completely, then frost with cream cheese frosting.

Frosting:
Cream butter and cream cheese, add confectioners sugar and beat until smooth. Add vanilla and nuts, mix completely and frost cake.

Shared by Susan Miller

Frosting:
1 stick butter or margarine, softened
8 ounces cream cheese, softened
1 box confectioners sugar
2 teaspoon vanilla
1 cup chopped pecans or walnuts

Cake:
1½ cups cooking oil
4 eggs
2 cups flour
2 cups sugar
2 teaspoons baking soda
2 teaspoons cinnamon
½ teaspoon salt
3 cups grated carrots

Susan's 14 Carrot Cake

*This cake is no fail and ever
so easy to make. A favorite
in our family. Enjoy!*

LAZY DAISY CAKE

Cake:
½ cup milk
1 tablespoon butter
1 teaspoon vanilla
1 cup sugar
2 eggs, well beaten
1 cup flour, sifted
1 teaspoon baking
   powder
pinch of salt

In a small saucepan, heat milk, butter and vanilla. In a large bowl, mix sugar and eggs. Add dry ingredients, sifted together. Add warmed milk mixture to egg mixture. Pour mixture into loaf pan. Bake for 30 minutes (until tester comes out clean) at 350°. Remove cake from oven and frost with the following frosting.

Frosting:
Heat all ingredients until sugar is melted. Spread on warm cake and put under broiler for a minute or two until lightly browned.

Frosting:
⅓ cup butter
⅔ cup brown sugar
½ cup coconut
4 tablespoons heavy
   cream

Shared by Dottie Cahill and Cari Sweitzer

Lazy Daisy Cake

BLACK BOTTOM PIES

8   cups Oreos
2   sticks butter
2½ gallons vanilla ice cream
4   cups fudge
¼   cup sliced almonds toasted

Blend Oreos in food processor and add melted butter. Mixture should be able to form a ball that holds together. Press approximately 1½ cups of crumb mixture into spring form pan. Cover bottom and ¾ of the height of the sides of pan with mixture. Bottom should be covered more heavily than the sides. Bake 5 minutes on 350°. Cool completely. Put extra crumbs aside for middle and topping of pie. Warm fudge in container until soft and spreadable. Let ice cream thaw partially so it is easy to spread. Fill cooled spring form pan half way with ice cream and sprinkle some crushed Oreo mixture on top of ice cream. Cover Oreo mixture with more ice cream until you reach ¼ inch from top of pan. Freeze for 30 minutes to chill and set. Remove from freezer and sprinkle with oreo mixture. Cover pie with 2 cups warm fudge. Don't go all the way to the top of the pan with the fudge as it will quickly overflow. Sprinkle the rest of crushed Oreos with toasted almonds on top of fudge, press down and freeze immediately. Makes 2 pies.

Shared by Ben Haberman from The Wharf

Black Bottom Pie

DELICIOUS DRINKS

The Madison Martini

Fuzzy Navel

Pink Panther

Lemon Slushie

To Die For Hot Chocolate

Blueberry Lemonade

Bill's Margarita

Honey Nana Smoothie

Grasshopper

Mango Madness

Strawberry Wine Cooler

Fresh Limeade with Rum

Homemade Eggnog

Raspberry Rum Fruit Punch

DELICIOUS DRINKS

THE MADISON MARTINI

2   ounces Gray Goose vodka
splash of cranberry juice

Shake with ice, pour promptly, garnish with a fresh flower skewer.

FUZZY NAVEL

1   shot vodka, chilled
2   shots of peach schnapps
½   cup freshly squeezed orange juice.

Shake with ice and serve in chilled glass, garnish with slice of orange.

PINK PANTHER

1   ounce pink lemonade
1   ounce citrus vodka

Shake and serve in chilled glass. Garnish.

Fuzzy Navel

Pink Panther

LEMON SLUSHIE

2   shots of citrus vodka, chilled
1   cup fresh lemonade
sugar to dip glass rim

Shake and serve in chilled glass with sugar around rim and garnish with lemon wedge.

TO DIE FOR HOT CHOCOLATE

2   cups milk
3   tablespoons hot chocolate mix
6   marshmallows

Heat milk in pot on stove. Bring to a simmer, not a boil. Take mugs, put a tablespoon of hot chocolate into each mug, and add a little of the warming milk to dissolve the powder. Add the marshmallows to mugs. When milk is simmering, pour into a container and shake to create frothy effect. Pour shaken, hot milk into mugs. Enjoy! Serves 2.

Lemon Slushie

BLUEBERRY LEMONADE

⅓ cup fresh lemon juice
2 cups water
2 cups fresh blueberries
½ cup sugar, add more if needed

Process all ingredients and pour through a strainer into a pitcher. Serve over ice and garnish with lemon slices.

BILL'S MARGARITA

2 shots of tequila, the good stuff
1 shot cointreau
1 shot freshly squeezed lime juice
salt for rim
lime wedge for serving

Shake and pour into glass. Serve promptly.

HONEY-NANA-SMOOTHIE

3 bananas
4 heaping tablespoons honey
1½ cup fat free yogurt–vanilla
ice cubes

Place all ingredients into blender and pulse.

Blueberry Lemonade

GRASSHOPPER

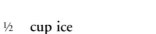

½   cup ice
1   ounce white Crème De Cacao
1   ounce Crème De Menthe
scoop of vanilla ice cream

Blend until smooth.

MANGO MADNESS

1   cup plain yogurt
½   cup mango juice, (jarred or canned) or 3 fresh
    mangos with juice, diced
5   teaspoons sugar
½   cup milk

Combine all ingredients in blender. Blend well and serve.

Grassshopper

STRAWBERRY WINE COOLER

2   cups fresh strawberries
⅓   cup sugar
1   bottle dry white wine, chilled

Combine strawberries and sugar and let marinade for ½ hour. Mix wine with strawberry mixture and blend until smooth. Strain with cheesecloth and pour into serving pitcher. Chill and serve over ice.

FRESH LIMEADE WITH RUM

1½ cups sugar
6   cups water
¾   cup lime juice
1   cup light rum

Combine sugar and 1 cup water and heat over medium heat. Bring to a boil, stirring constantly. Cool. Stir in the rest of the water, lime juice and rum. Mix and pour into a metal bowl, cover and freeze for about 2 hours. Keep breaking up the ice as it forms. Transfer to serving pitcher and keep cold.

HOMEMADE EGGNOG

12 extra large eggs
1½ cups sugar
2   quarts half and half
4   cups bourbon
1   cup dark rum
nutmeg

Separate all 12 eggs, placing yolks in separate bowl from the whites. Beat egg whites on high speed, slowly adding 1 cup of the sugar. Beat until whites peak. Beat yolks on high speed slowly adding remaining ½ cup of sugar. Beat until thick and creamy. Fold the whites and yolks together until mixed thoroughly. Carefully add half and half, bourbon and rum to the egg mixture. Refrigerate. Serve in small cups, over ice if desired. Sprinkle with nutmeg.

Shared by Barbara Gibbons

RASPBERRY RUM FRUIT PUNCH

8   ounces raspberry puree
2   cups Minute Maid blends–Orange Passion
2   cups pineapple juice
2   tablespoons fresh lemon juice
1½ cups rum

To make puree, put 2 cups fresh or frozen raspberries in blender and mix until thick and smooth. Combine all.

INDEX

CONNOR. HALLE. JOHNNY. TY. JULIE. JESSE. CAROLYN

Our kids

Our inspiration

ACKNOWLEDGEMENTS

We dedicate this book to our mothers, LorettaTallevast and
Phyllis Carroll for inspiring a passion for cooking
in us early on.

To our husbands for their patience and love.

To John Carroll, who has forever encouraged women in
business and has offered his wisdom and support to us.

A special thank you to Kelley McMahon who is responsible for all
the beautiful photography you have seen throughout this book.
And to Lisa Kronauer for her artisitc creativity and her willingness
to donate her time.